J.

THE
1980s

Other books in this series:

THE
1980s

James D. Torr, *Book Editor*

David L. Bender, *Publisher*
Bruno Leone, *Executive Editor*
Bonnie Szumski, *Series Editor*
David M. Haugen, *Managing Editor*

Greenhaven Press, Inc., San Diego, California

AMERICA'S DECADES

Every effort has been made to trace the owners of copyrighted material. The articles in this volume may have been edited for content, length, and/or reading level. The titles have been changed to enhance the editorial purpose.

No part of this book may be reproduced or used in any form or by any means, electrical, mechanical, or otherwise, including, but not limited to, photocopy, recording, or any information storage and retrieval system, without prior written permission from the publisher.

Library of Congress Cataloging-in-Publication Data

The 1980s / James D. Torr, book editor.
        p.   cm. — (America's decades)
     Includes bibliographical references and index.
     ISBN 0-7377-0310-5 (lib. : acid-free paper) —
     ISBN 0-7377-0309-1 (pbk. : acid-free paper)
     1. United States—Civilization—1970– . 2. Nineteen eighties.
  I. Torr, James D., 1974–   . II. Series.

  E169.12 .A175 2000
  973.92—dc21   99-055864
                                                        CIP

Cover photo: (top) Joan Slatkin/Archive Photos,
(bottom) © Peter Turnley
Terry Arthur/White House, 102
AT&T, 155
NASA, 163

©2000 by Greenhaven Press, Inc.
P.O. Box 289009, San Diego, CA 92198-9009

Printed in the U.S.A.

Contents

Chapter 1: The Reagan Revolution

1. The Origins of '80s Conservatism
by Iwan W. Morgan   34
Jimmy Carter's presidency was plagued with problems,
including economic recession, an energy crisis, and the
Soviet invasion of Afghanistan. The Republican Party
capitalized on Carter's failure to resolve the Iran
hostage crisis, and the public elected Ronald Reagan to
the White House.

2. Reagan's Policies Shape American Politics
by George Moss   44
The Reagan administration worked to lower government spending on social programs, cut taxes, and reduce federal regulations on industry and the environment. Reagan also appointed several conservative
justices to the Supreme Court.

3. The Truth About the 1980s Economy
by Michael Schaller   52
Conservatives view the economic growth of the 1980s
as a source of pride, while liberals are just as quick to
argue that Reagan's policies benefited only the rich.
Both claims have some merit: Many but not all groups
prospered in the 1980s, while the federal deficit soared.

4. The 1984 Election: The Height of Reagan's
Popularity *by William H. Chafe*   61
Dubbed the "Great Communicator" and the "Teflon
president," Reagan was one of the most politically popular presidents of the twentieth century. This was most
evident in the 1984 presidential election, in which Reagan cruised to an easy victory against Democratic candidate Walter Mondale.

the fall of the Berlin Wall that divided East and West
Germany.

Chapter 3: Science and Society

the Vietnam War. Early 1980s films such as *Rambo* appealed to those who felt the war should have been won, while later movies such as *Platoon* and *Full Metal Jacket* portrayed a darker, soldier's-eye view of the war.

Foreword

In his book *The American Century*, historian Harold Evans maintains that the history of the twentieth century has been dominated by the rise of the United States as a global power: "The British dominated the nineteenth century, and the Chinese may cast a long shadow on the twenty-first, but the twentieth century belongs to the United States." In a 1998 interview he summarized his sweeping hypothesis this way: "At the beginning of the century the number of free democratic nations in the world was very limited. Now, at the end of the century, democracy is ascendant around the globe, and America has played the major part in making that happen."

As the new century dawns, historians are eager to appraise the past one hundred years. Evans's book is just one of many attempts to assess the historical impact that the United States has had in the past century. Although not all historians agree with Evans's characterization of the twentieth century as "America's century," no one disputes his basic observation that "in only the second century of its existence the United States became the world's leading economic, military and cultural power." For most of the twentieth century the United States has played an increasingly larger role in shaping world events. The Greenhaven Press America's Decades series is designed to help readers develop a better understanding of America and Americans during this important time.

Each volume in the ten-volume series provides an in-depth examination of the time period. In compiling each volume, editors have striven to cover not only the defining events of the decade—in both the domestic and international arenas—but also the cultural, intellectual, and technological trends that affected people's everyday lives.

Essays in the America's Decades series have been chosen for their concise, accessible, and engaging presentation of the facts. Each selection is preceded by a summary of the article's content. A comprehensive index and an annotated table of contents also aid readers in quickly locating material of interest. Each volume begins with an introductory essay that presents the broader themes of each decade. Several research aids are also present, including an extensive bibliography and a timeline that provides an at-a-glance overview of each decade.

Each volume in the Greenhaven Press America's Decades series serves as an informative introduction to a specific period in U.S. history. Together, the volumes comprise a detailed overview of twentieth century American history and serve as a valuable resource for students conducting research on this fascinating time period.

Introduction: Assessing the 1980s

In 1980, America's ideological Cold War with the Soviet Union was in full swing, and the Berlin Wall stood as a symbol of the division between Western and Eastern Europe. Few people had ever used computers. Fewer still had heard of the Internet, compact discs, VCRs, or microwave ovens, and no one had ever heard of AIDS. By 1990, the world was a very different place.

As historians debate the significance of all the changes that occurred in the 1980s, individuals and the government are still trying to cope with them. The rapid growth of computers and the Internet has had a profound effect on America's national economy as well as people's daily lives. On a more global scale, the end of the Cold War, the most dominant force in international relations since the end of World War II, has left the nations of the former Soviet Union struggling to rebuild both their economies and their national identities. At the same time, the United States is reevaluating its foreign policies now that America is, as many commentators put it after the Soviet Union began to disintegrate in 1989, "the world's only remaining superpower."

The 1970s: A Decade of Discontent

Every period in American history has been strongly influenced by the events that preceded it, and the 1980s are no exception. Historians interpret many of the political and cultural developments of the 1980s primarily as reactions to events that occurred in previous decades, especially the 1970s.

The 1970s is widely viewed as a troubled time in American history. Political scandals and a poor economy at home, as well as the Vietnam War and other foreign policy problems abroad, have all contributed to this characterization.

No issue shaped the 1970s more than the Vietnam War. American troops had been fighting Communist encroachment in Vietnam since 1965, and opposition to the war grew throughout the late 1960s as television coverage exposed more and more Americans to the brutality of the conflict. In 1968, Richard Nixon succeeded Lyndon Johnson as president. When first elected, Nixon had promised to end U.S. involvement in Vietnam; thus many Americans were outraged to learn in 1973 that Nixon had expanded American involvement in the war, secretly condoning the bombing of neutral Cambodia.

Controversy over Vietnam continued well past the war's end in 1975. Many Americans regarded the conflict in Vietnam as a national disgrace, while others viewed the antiwar movement with contempt, believing that the United States could have succeeded in Vietnam if Americans had been more supportive of the government during the conflict. When Reagan took office in 1980, he attributed many of America's problems to the distrust and uncertainty caused by what he called the "Vietnam syndrome."

Watergate Tarnishes the Presidency

Political scandals in the 1970s compounded the antigovernment sentiment surrounding Vietnam. Nixon and his Republican running mate, Spiro Agnew, had been elected in 1968, and they were reelected by a wide margin in 1972. However, nine months after their inauguration, Agnew pleaded no contest to charges of income tax evasion, resigned, and was replaced by Republican congressman Gerald Ford. Agnew's resignation foreshadowed Nixon's own after the infamous Watergate scandal.

On June 17, 1972, five men were arrested and charged with burglary at the Democratic National Headquarters at the Watergate Hotel in Washington, D.C. The men had ties to the president and had broken in to repair one of the Nixon administration's wiretaps. (As the Watergate incident wore on, it was revealed that, throughout his presidency, Nixon had engaged in illegal wiretapping of people he considered enemies—for example, opponents of the war in Vietnam.) Hoping to avoid a scandal in an election year, Nixon ordered a cover-up of the incident.

The cover-up eventually backfired. After a lengthy series of investigations, accusations, and indictments that demoralized the nation, many of the Nixon administration's illegal activities were revealed. In 1974 a grand jury named Nixon as a coconspirator in the cover-up. Facing almost certain impeachment, he resigned, and on August 8, 1974, Gerald Ford became president.

Together, Watergate and Vietnam had a devastating impact on the nation's morale. The feelings these events fostered among the American public—loss of faith in elected officials and serious distrust of government in general—continue to haunt Americans. In the 1980s, when Ronald Reagan became embroiled in his own political scandal, the Iran-contra affair, few could help but compare it to Watergate, and when Reagan sent troops to Beirut, Lebanon, and provided military aid to Nicaragua and El Salvador, critics feared that these actions would escalate into "another Vietnam." Similar fears resurfaced in 1991 when George Bush sent troops to the Persian Gulf.

"National Malaise"

The poor economy of the 1970s only exacerbated the problems facing the nation. Workers' incomes had gone into decline by the mid-1970s, and would not rise again for years. At the same time, seemingly uncontrollable inflation was causing prices to rise. Gasoline shortages—imposed by the leaders of the Middle East who control much of the world's oil—curtailed any leisure activity that involved an automobile, and made Americans acutely aware of limits of their nation's influence in the world.

As he finished out Nixon's second term, Gerald Ford could do little to alleviate the pessimism that pervaded the nation. Many Americans were also angered when Ford granted Nixon a full pardon a month after his resignation. It was no surprise when he lost the 1976 presidential election to the Democratic challenger, Jimmy Carter.

In the wake of Watergate, Carter was able to use as his campaign slogan a simple promise: "I'll never tell a lie."

Unfortunately, Carter was unable to resolve the problems of inflation and unemployment that plagued the economy, and another gas shortage in 1979 only made matters worse. All these problems contributed to what Carter called a "national malaise" that pervaded society during his tenure in office.

Carter did, however, win international recognition for his role in the historic Middle East peace treaty of 1978—the Camp David Accords, as they came to be known, are regarded as his greatest achievement. And on the issue of Vietnam, Carter tended to embrace the view of those who felt the war had been largely a mistake. However, the pacifist image these views fostered eventually backfired on Carter.

On November 4, 1979, thousands of revolutionaries stormed the American embassy in Tehran, Iran. Fifty-three Americans were taken hostage. Carter put political and economic pressure on the terrorists, and even ordered a rescue attempt, but these measures were unsuccessful. Of all the problems that plagued the Carter administration, the Iran hostage crisis proved to be the most damaging. In 1980, with the hostages still held captive, Republican challenger Ronald Reagan characterized Carter as weak and ineffectual, and voters agreed that new leadership was needed.

"Morning in America"

Ronald Reagan had been a former movie actor in the late 1930s and early 1940s, starring in films such as *King's Row* and *For God and Country*. He earned the nickname "the Gipper" for the role he played in his most popular film, *Knute Rockne, All American*. In the late 1940s and early 1950s, after he became involved in a dispute over communism within the film industry, Reagan's views shifted from liberal to conservative. He joined the Republican Party in 1962, and won the governorship of California in 1966.

In his 1980 run for president, Reagan promised to improve the economy and restore America's reputation as a global leader. His campaign commercials proclaimed "it's morning in America," implying that in the 1980s the nation would awake from the malaise of the 1970s. Whereas Carter had called on Americans to sacrifice—by limiting their consumption of oil and gas in order to deal with the energy crisis—Reagan promised a tax cut. In the end he ousted the incumbent Carter, garnering 51 percent of the popular vote.

In his first term in office Reagan became one of the most popular presidents in history. An example of Reagan's ability to endear himself to the nation was his graceful handling of an assassination attempt on March 30, 1981, just over two months after he was inaugurated. The president was shot and gravely wounded, but as doctors rushed to examine him he quipped to his wife, "Honey, I forgot to duck." Later he joked to the doctors about to operate on him, "I hope you're all Republicans." As Haynes Johnson, author of *Sleepwalking Through History: America in the Reagan Years*, explains:

> These remarks, when instantly relayed to the press, understandably had a powerful and positive effect on the American public. The subsequent cheerfulness and grace Reagan displayed during his long recovery in hospital and White House, his ritual waves and smiles . . . all conveyed a sense to the public that Reagan possessed larger-than-life qualities. . . . Reagan's survival alone was proof enough that the country's luck had turned for the better.[1]

Former Speaker of the House "Tip" O'Neill explained Reagan's popularity this way: "They're rooting for him because we haven't had any presidential successes for years—Kennedy killed, Johnson with Vietnam, Nixon with Watergate, Ford, Carter, and all the rest."[2] "Without a doubt Reagan restored the heroic image of the presidency,"[3] agrees British historian Iwan W. Morgan. Reagan was the first president to serve a full two terms since Dwight D. Eisenhower left office in 1961, reflecting the seeming stability that he brought to the office and the nation.

"He mastered the art of media politics," writes historian

George Moss, "Nicknamed the Great Communicator, he used television skillfully to sell himself and his conservative program to the majority of the electorate."[4] "To a degree unmatched in any era since Franklin Roosevelt's New Deal, Ronald Reagan imprinted his own personal brand on the decade of the 1980s,"[5] writes historian William H. Chafe. His enormous influence on America in the 1980s is evident in the most popular epithet for the decade: "the Reagan era."

On November 6, 1984, Reagan was reelected by the widest electoral college margin in U.S. history, reaffirming his remarkable personal popularity. However, public support for the Reagan administration did wane somewhat during his second term. The event that was most damaging to Reagan personally was the Iran-contra scandal, in which Reagan officials were accused of selling arms to terrorists in Iran and illegally funding the contras, a rebel group in Nicaragua, in order to further the Reagan administration's own political goals. Yet Americans in the 1980s were remarkably reluctant to blame this scandal, or other problems, such as the stock market crash of October 16, 1987, on the president himself. In addition to the "Great Communicator," the media referred to Reagan as the "Teflon president" for his ability to deflect controversy about the problems the nation faced throughout the 1980s.

The New Conservatism

The popular press immediately heralded Reagan's 1980 victory as the beginning of the "Reagan Revolution." The term, in the words of historians John E. Findling and Frank W. Thackeray, "reflects the perception that the presidency of Ronald Reagan . . . represented a significant change in the philosophy that governed federal policymaking."[6] Specifically, writes Harold Evans in his book *The American Century*, the election of Reagan in 1980 and 1984, and of George Bush in 1988, marked "an ascendancy of conservative political doctrine."[7]

Evans also notes that the simple term "conservative" does not adequately describe the political philosophy that dominated the 1980s. "The terms 'liberal' and 'conservative' are political spaghetti," he writes, "liberal and conservative have meant different things at different times in American history."[8] For Reagan, Bush, and other mainstream Republicans in the 1980s, conservatism incorporated the beliefs of two principle groups: economic libertarians on the one hand, who advocated a smaller, less intrusive government, and moral conservatives on the other, who advocated family values and were strongly opposed to abortion, drug use, and communism, all of which they associated with liberalism.

Thus Reagan's primary goals as he entered office were to reduce the size of the federal government through massive budget cuts—which would allow him to both lower taxes and return more authority to the states—and to expand the military so that the United States would be able to negotiate with the Soviet Union from a position of strength. Reagan also voiced support for conservative ideals such as commitment to religion and family.

Supply-Side Economics

The economic agenda of the New Right, as the conservatives that supported Reagan were called, was the most "revolutionary" part of the Reagan plan. Ever since Franklin Delano Roosevelt's New Deal in the 1930s, under which many large government programs such as Social Security were created to help Americans recover from the Great Depression, there had been a widespread consensus that regulating industry and providing aid to the elderly and the poor were all legitimate functions of government. This consensus was evident in the 1960s, when Lyndon Johnson instituted his Great Society legislation, which, among other things, created Medicare, the government health insurance plan for the elderly.

Reagan and the New Right challenged this consensus. They believed that the welfare state had become too powerful and bureaucratic. In his first inaugural speech, Reagan proclaimed, "It is time to check the growth of government which shows signs of having grown beyond the consent of the governed."[9] They argued, for example, that the high taxes required to pay for social programs had slowed economic growth, and that government welfare programs undermined poor people's incentive to work.

The cornerstone of Reagan's plan to reduce government spending and revive the economy was known as supply-side economics. It was quickly dubbed "Reaganomics" by the media. At its core was the idea that if corporations and the wealthy are taxed less, they will invest more and help boost the economy, and all segments of society will benefit. To implement supply-side theory, Reagan appointed former Republican congressman David Stockman as director of the Office of Budget Management. Historian William H. Chafe summarizes Stockman's goals:

> Sharp reduction in income taxes, Stockman believed, would encourage savings and investments; deregulation of industry, in turn, would free business to compete more efficiently in the marketplace; rolling back environmental protection measures would release energy and resources for private development; and cutting back social expenditures to the old and the poor would bolster self-reliance and initiative. The overall goal, Stockman later said, was "a minimalist government . . . a spare and stingy creature which offered even-handed public justice, but no more." Millions might suffer in the short run, but in the long run, America would be strengthened "by abruptly severing the umbilical cords of dependency that ran from Washington to every nook and cranny of the nation."[10]

That the Reagan administration favored a smaller, "stingier" government angered many liberals, who felt that cutting welfare and other social programs showed a lack of compassion for the needy. They condemned Reaganomics, charging that Reagan's tax cuts and other policies favored the rich at the expense of the poor. The day after Reagan's election in 1980, Democratic senator Paul Tsongas lamented the nation's willingness to accept Reagan's ideas: "Basically," he said, "the New Deal died yesterday."[11] In a 1984 speech, New York governor Mario Cuomo charged that "Reagan made the denial of compassion acceptable" and that Reagan's attack on the welfare state "gave the middle class a reason not to care about the poor."[12]

Market Culture

The view that Americans had become uncaring was compounded by the fact that the rich did get richer in the 1980s. Reagan signed his major tax cut, the Economic Recovery Tax Act, in 1981. Due to Reagan's initiatives and other factors involving the global economy, states Iwan Morgan,

> By 1984 the economy was booming, the rise of 6.8 percent in GNP being the highest annual increase since 1951. The beneficiaries were mostly the wealthy. The richest 1 percent of Americans owned 14.9 percent of the national wealth by 1988, compared with 8 percent in 1980. The middle classes also did well out of "Reaganomics," which helped create a new class of young, upwardly mobile professionals, the so-called yuppies. However, . . . poverty was manifestly on the increase, rather than on the decline. According to official statistics, 14.4 percent of Americans were poor in 1984, compared with 11 percent in 1979.[13]

Disputes over the economic policies of the 1980s continued well past the decade's end, with some observers arguing that the wealth did eventually "trickle-down" to lower income groups as the 1980s wore on. Thus conservatives argue that the healthy economy of the 1990s was due to Reagan's initiatives, while liberals flatly reject this claim. Whatever the case, there was a growing concern throughout the 1980s that the gap between rich and poor was widening.

The extravagant shows of wealth that characterized 1980s' culture no doubt contributed to this feeling. Cultural commentators cite 1980s' TV shows such as *Dallas* and *Lifestyles of the Rich and Famous*, as well as Madonna's hit song "Material Girl," as evidence of America's preoccupation with wealth. But the media in the 1980s were already preoccupied with the trend: *Newsweek* proclaimed 1984 "The Year of the Yuppie," an acronym for young, urban, upwardly mobile professionals, who showed their wealth with expensive clothes, cars, apartments, and electronics. David Wright describes the yuppie phenomenon in his book *America in the Twentieth Century: 1980–1989*:

> [Yuppies] annoyed the rest of the population in different ways. Older and less affluent Americans considered them ostentatious. Cars such as BMWs became symbols of excess to people who were trying to patch together aging Chevys or Fords. On college campuses, "Die yuppie scum!" became a popular bumper sticker. But there were many collegians eagerly awaiting their chance to become urban professionals too.[14]

Critics of the growing obsession with wealth cite several high-profile incidents in which wealthy individuals attempted to become even wealthier through illegal activities. Michael Milken made millions selling high-risk "junk" bonds and used the money to finance corporate takeovers, until he was finally implicated in several insider-trading scandals and convicted of fraud and racketeering in 1987. Ivan Boesky, another one of Wall Street's most famous traders, advocated "merger mania"—as the controversial wave of corporate buyouts in the 1980s was known—then was convicted of insider-trading charges in 1986. That same year, in a now-infamous speech to the graduating business students at the University of California at Berkeley, Boesky assured students that in a free market society, "greed is healthy."

A Decade of Greed?

All this has led many to characterize the 1980s as a decade of greed. As the economy went into recession in 1990, news magazines were filled with articles such as *Business Week*'s "Was the Last Decade Really So Cruel: Yes," the *New York Times Magazine*'s "Reagan's America: A Capital Offense," and *Newsweek*'s "The 1980s: Market Culture Run Amok." More conservative periodicals were quick to respond with their own economic analyses, especially when the economy rebounded in 1992. Richard B. McKenzie's 1993 book *What Went Right in the 1980s* is emblematic of this trend. However appropriate or inappropriate the "decade of greed" view may be, it is important to note how widespread the sentiment was as the 1980s drew to a close, and how it affected the politics of the 1990s.

In retrospect, many observers have noted that the conservative shift in American politics was not as dramatic as conservatives had hoped and liberals had feared that it would be. For one thing, a Democrat was back in office by 1992. Findling and Thackeray write:

> In November 1988, the Reagan Revolution was passed on to George Bush, Reagan's vice president. . . . Although Bush generally carried on Reagan's economic policies . . . he did not have the charisma that carried Reagan to such heights of popularity. . . . Bush failed in his bid for reelection in 1992, losing to Bill Clinton, the governor of Arkansas. After twelve years, the Reagan Revolution was over.[15]

But many conservatives also lament that Reagan did not accomplish his stated fiscal goal of reducing the size of government. As policy analyst John Robson notes:

> Despite a lot of rhetoric from both the administration and its critics, domestic spending under Reagan went up; the share of the Gross National Product (GNP) taken by the federal government went up; the deficit went up; entitlements expanded. . . . On policy and legislative questions, the Reagan Revolution saw the state intervening ever more deeply into the economy.[16]

In this view, then, Reagan did not truly abandon the New Deal as many had predicted in 1980, since he did not eliminate either Medicare or Social Security, two of the largest and most popular federal programs. Spending increased while taxes decreased, and the federal deficit soared: In the

1980s, the United States went from being the world's largest creditor to the world's largest debtor. The high rate of federal spending was partly due to the fact that defense spending nearly doubled during Reagan's first term, from $134 billion in 1980 to $252 billion in 1985.

Reagan Revives the Cold War

Although unable to fully implement his domestic agenda, Reagan exerted an enormous influence over U.S. foreign policy throughout his two terms in office. "[Reagan's] foreign policy was simple and direct: It rested entirely on opposing the Soviet Union,"[17] writes Cold War historian Walter LaFeber. William H. Chafe maintains that "If there was one single theme that had dominated Ronald Reagan's public pronouncements from 1947 until the end of his second term in office, it was his evangelical denunciation of communism, and his complete identification of American patriotism with anti-Sovietism."[18] In a famous 1982 speech, Reagan denounced the Soviet Union as an "evil empire" and "the focus of evil in the modern world."

Yet despite his hostility toward communism, Reagan in his second term became part of one of the most dramatic turning points of the twentieth century, as tensions between the United States and the Soviet Union first rose, then quickly relaxed into a mood of mutual cooperation that once seemed unthinkable.

Since the end of World War II, the Cold War—the ideological conflict between, on the one hand, the United States and other capitalist nations of the West, and, on the other, the Communist Soviet Union and its allies—had dominated global politics. Throughout the 1950s—for example, in the Korean War—the United States had followed the credo of the Truman Doctrine, opposing the development of communism in noncommunist countries. However, with the quagmire in Vietnam, Richard Nixon and his national security advisor and later secretary of state, Henry Kissinger, reasoned that "the United States could no longer sustain the burden of containing the expansion of international communism by military means,"[19] as historian Joseph Smith puts it. Instead, Nixon sought friendlier relations with the Soviet Union. The policy of seeking a relaxation of tensions was known as détente.

The Reagan Doctrine

Reagan rejected détente. In what became known as the Reagan Doctrine, the United States renewed its opposition to the spread of communism. Peter B. Levy, author of the *Encyclopedia of the Reagan-Bush Years*, describes the logic of the Reagan Doctrine this way: "Since the United Sates was committed to containing communism . . . it should provide support for anticommunist regimes, even if they were not democratically run, and to anticommunist insurgents in the developing world."[20] Under this policy, the Reagan administration provided military aid to the rebel contras in their effort to overthrow the Marxist government of Nicaragua, and to the government of El Salvador in their efforts to crush Communist insurgents.

Under the Reagan Doctrine the United States also initiated a massive military buildup. In the 1980 campaign Reagan warned that the Soviet Union was winning the arms race; as president he engaged in protracted battles with Congress over building new weapons systems such as the MX missile and B-1 bomber. His most controversial proposal was the Strategic Defense Initiative: In 1983, in a nationally televised address, Reagan announced plans for a space-based, computer controlled defense that would shoot down nuclear missiles before they reached their targets. Walter LaFeber writes:

> Pentagon advisors had long discounted the possibility of 'Star Wars,' as this proposal was labeled. Reagan ignored them and also most American scientists, who believed that such a defense was not only impossible to build but dangerous to even suggest, because it could destabilize both U.S. and Soviet faith in mutual deterrence. The Soviets, for example, might build many times more missiles so they could simply overwhelm any Star Wars defense.[21]

As LaFeber notes, the weapons system was never built, but the reactions that Reagan's announcement provoked did serve to increase worldwide tensions about nuclear war. Russian leader Yuri Andropov warned that the United States was embarking upon "an extremely dangerous path."[22]

A Sudden Thaw

To almost everyone's surprise, the relationship between the two superpowers quickly began to change after 1985. "Neither the Soviet Union nor the outside world could have foreseen the historic consequences that would flow from the election of Mikhail Gorbachev on March 11, 1985,"[23] writes journalist Dan Oberdorfer in his book *From the Cold War to a New Era*. Much younger than the Soviet leaders that had preceded him, Gorbachev was convinced that the Soviet Union was in serious need of reform. He advocated glasnost, the Russian word for *openness*, in both the Soviet Union itself and its relations with the West.

To the surprise of many who viewed Reagan as an intractable "cold warrior," writes Cold War scholar John Lewis Gaddis, the president "welcomed the fresh breezes emanating from Moscow and moved quickly to establish a personal relationship with the new Soviet leader."[24] A series of historic arms control summit meetings followed. These talks began at Geneva, Switzerland, in 1985 and culminated in December 1987 in Washington, D.C., when the two leaders signed the Intermediate-range Nuclear Forces (INF) Treaty, agreeing to destroy an entire class of nuclear missiles. That summit also changed many Americans views about their Cold War rivals, as the American media became fascinated with Gorbachev and his wife, Raisa.

Gorbachev's leadership greatly changed the way Americans and the world viewed the Soviet Union, but the effect he had on his own nation was even more profound. To revive the stagnant Soviet economy, Gorbachev initiated economic reforms known as perestroika, the Russian word for *restructuring*, and criticized the corruption within the *nomenklatura*, or the Soviet ruling class. Yet his actions had unintended consequences in the satellite nations of Eastern Europe that had been under Soviet control for decades. Joseph Smith writes, "The introduction of glasnost and perestroika in the Soviet Union stimulated movements for the same fundamental reforms in Eastern Europe. In the process, the power and authority of local communist bosses were seriously challenged and swept away."[25]

The Revolutions of 1989

Consistent with his desire for a more "open" Russia, Gorbachev allowed these reform movements to proceed in a democratic manner. One by one, anticommunist movements arose within Poland, Hungary, Czechoslovakia, Bulgaria, East Germany, and Romania. These prodemocracy movements gained much more momentum, however, than Gorbachev had anticipated. Martin Walker, in *The Cold War: A History*, writes, "Once Gorbachev had opened a space for the peoples of Eastern Europe to exploit, they poured into it and through it, seizing the chance of determining their own destiny for the first time since 1939."[26]

Walker calls 1989 the "Year of Miracles," for in that one year Poland, Hungary, Czechoslovakia, East Germany, and Bulgaria all rejected Communist rule. The most poignant scene in this historic year occurred on November 9, 1989, when East Germany opened the Berlin Wall and it was subsequently torn down by jubilant crowds. "The exhilaration generated by the fall of the Berlin Wall . . . is beyond description. In that one night the entire picture of Europe constructed in the mind of almost all its citizens for forty years underwent an irreversible phase shift,"[27] writes historian Gale Stokes.

It was George Bush rather than Reagan who led America through the "Year of Miracles." His response to the events of 1989 was surprisingly restrained. For example, when Poland requested $10 billion in U.S. aid to help the nation through its transition away from communism, and Bush's reply was noncommittal, Polish intellectual Adam Michnik accused the Bush administration of "sleepwalking through history."[28] The former president's defenders insist that any U.S. intervention at such a crucial time might be misinterpreted by the Soviets; Bush was careful not to boast about having "won" the Cold War.

Nevertheless, writes Iwan Morgan, "in 1990, President Bush pronounced the Cold War over," and commentaries on the events in Eastern Europe became dominated by an "'end-of-history' theory, according to which liberal democracy's triumph over communism signifies the end of the ideological conflict that had shaped world history in the twentieth century."[29] These views were strengthened in 1991 by the final disintegration of the Soviet Union into its constituent republics.

Life in the '80s

While historians will no doubt remember the 1980s for these earth-shattering events, Americans who lived through the 1980s may be more likely to recall the developments that impacted their everyday lives. For example, as the threat of Communist expansion decreased, Americans worried more about other problems, such as terrorism, drug use, and AIDS.

AIDS first appeared in 1981, and by the end of 1982, 750 cases had been reported in the United States and almost 1,600 worldwide. By the mid-1980s fear of AIDS had gripped the nation: In one famous example Ryan White, a thirteen-year-old hemophiliac who had contracted HIV through a blood transfusion, was barred from attending school. The disease was also strongly associated with gay men, and exacerbated many people's antihomosexual sentiments.

Alvin and Virginia Silverstein open their 1986 book *AIDS: Deadly Threat*, with a dire prediction that is indicative of many people's fears in the 1980s: "Future generations may look back at the 1980s as the 'AIDS decade' when a new deadly disease first emerged as worldwide threat."[30] Yet Mirko D. Grmek, in his book *History of AIDS*, notes "The first AIDS patients . . . triggered fear and prejudice disproportionate to their numbers."[31] Whatever the case, the disease certainly changed the nation's attitudes towards sex: "'Safe sex' became a code phrase for 'use condoms,'"[32] writes author Myron A. Marty, and he notes that around the same time television stations and magazines abandoned their restrictions on advertising condoms.

Both Problems and Signs of Progress

AIDS was certainly not the only problem making headlines. Estimates of homelessness reached record highs in 1986. Americans in that same year also witnessed the explosion of the space shuttle *Challenger*, the Chernobyl nuclear power plant disaster, and the announcement by President and Nancy Reagan of their "Just Say No" to drugs campaign, in response to increased use of crack cocaine and other drugs. Farmers in the early 1980s experienced hard times as a result of drought and a depressed world economy. And on October 19, 1987, the stock market took its largest one-day plunge in history, sending waves of panic throughout Wall Street. In the area of the environment, the decade began with the eruption of the Mount St. Helens volcano in 1980, and ended in 1989 with the *Exxon Valdez* oil spill, the worst in U.S. history.

But there were many positive developments for Americans in the 1980s. As more women entered the workforce than ever before, they made some important gains: In 1981 the Supreme Court ruled that a woman could sue her employer for receiving less pay than a man who performed the same work, and in the 1984 election Democratic presidential candidate Walter Mondale selected Geraldine Ferraro as his running mate, making her the first woman to run for the office on a major party's ticket.

In the realm of technology, personal computers, regarded as expensive novelty items in the 1970s, were fueling a $70 billion-a-year industry by 1990, and could be found in homes, classrooms, and offices throughout the nation. The "PC revolution" of the 1980s set the stage for the development of the Internet and the "information revolution" of the 1990s.

Electronic Culture

As for the culture of the 1980s, Americans enjoyed more entertainment options than ever before. The VCR gave rise to the home video, allowing people to watch more movies at home; the rapid growth of cable television resulted in more television stations. One new station, Music Television (MTV), spawned a new musical format for the recording industry, the music video. And the number of books and magazines being published increased throughout the 1980s.

On network television, *The Cosby Show* was the decade's most popular program, ranked number one in the Nielsen ratings every year from 1984 through 1992. Some observers have interpreted this fact as a positive indicator of race relations in the 1980s, since the sitcom concerns a black family. Others believe the show's popularity lies with its portrayal of two major themes of the 1980s: family values and affluence. Linda K. Fuller, author of a book on the program's success, notes, "*The Cosby Show* has become well engrained in our popular culture as synonymous with the ideal family, the one we all wish we were a part of," and that "not only are both parents professionals, but also their forebears appear to have been monied. Tidbits from family stories and old friends' reminisces let us know that this Black family has been upwardly mobile for a long time."[33]

In popular music, the punk music phenomenon of the 1970s gave way to the new wave and heavy metal genres of the early 1980s. Later in the decade, rap music gained mainstream popularity. There were some indications that the music industry was becoming more socially responsible, as events such as Live Aid, a "mega-concert" held simultaneously in London, Philadelphia, and Sydney, raised $67 million for starving Africans. Farm Aid and similar benefit concerts soon followed.

Many critics' assessments of 1980s' culture can be summed up by film reviewer Richard Schickel's comments about the cinema of the decade: "A handful of great movies, two handfuls of interesting movies, and a lot of stuff it's impossible to remember or care about."[34] Fantasy and science fiction were the themes of some of the most popular movies. Steven Spielberg's *E.T.: The Extra-Terrestrial* (1982) was the top-grossing film of the decade. Other blockbuster hits included the last two films of the *Star Wars* (1979) saga, *The Empire Strikes Back* (1980) and *Return of the Jedi* (1983), as well as *Raiders of the Lost Ark* (1981), *Ghostbusters* (1984), and *Batman* (1989).

But many students of popular culture value other films of the 1980s for their ability to mirror trends in society. For example, author William Palmer notes how movies of the era reflected changing Cold War tensions:

> The fascination of eighties American films with Russian themes closely followed the contour of the historical rhetoric of America-Russian relations. Early, films like *Red Dawn* and the TV series *Amerika* examined the differences between the society and ideologies, their potentials for brutality towards each other. By mid-decade, films like *Rocky IV* and *White Nights* had taken up the Reagan "evil empire" patriotic jingoism. But after the 1985 Geneva summit, Hollywood had to scramble to accommodate the sudden change in rhetoric. . . . Films like *Little Nikita*, *Russkies*, and *Red Heat* underlined that rhetorical shift.[35]

Louis Giannetti and Scott Eyman, authors of *Flashback: A Brief History of Film*, write, "The decade was dominated by the conservative ideology of President Ronald Reagan, a former movie star. Mainstream Hollywood films reflected many of Reagan's values, especially nationalism, winning, money, family solidarity, and militarism."[36] David Brode notes in *The Movies of the Eighties* that "Hollywood quickly adopted [Reagan's] old-fashioned flag-waving attitudes. In *Superman II*, Christopher Reeve carries the red, white and blue ever upward; in *Rocky IV*, Stallone literally draped himself in the American flag."[37]

Looking Back

The significance of many of these trends in 1980s' culture is only evident in retrospect. Likewise, historians are only beginning to understand what the lasting impact of the 1980s will be. Debate rages, for example, over what the long-term effects of Reaganomics will be, or how global politics will be affected by the collapse of the Soviet Union. "The Reagan era," "morning in America," "the end of history," "a decade of greed": All are attempts to capture the essence of an era, but the decade continues to resist such easy classification. The phrase, "only time will tell" certainly applies when assessing the legacy of the 1980s.

1. Haynes Johnson, *Sleepwalking Through History: America in the Reagan Years*. New York: W.W. Norton, 1991.

2. Quoted in Susan Jeffords, *Hard Bodies: Hollywood Masculinity in the Reagan Era*. New Brunswick, NJ: Rutgers University Press, 1994, p. 23.

3. Iwan W. Morgan, "The Age of Uncertainty: The United States Since 1973," in Iwan W. Morgan and Neil A. Wynn, eds., *America's Century: Perspectives on U.S. History Since 1900*. New York: Holmes & Meier, 1993, p. 207.

4. George Moss, *America in the Twentieth Century*. Englewood Cliffs, NJ: Prentice-Hall, 1989, p. 434.

5. William H. Chafe, *The Unfinished Journey: America Since World War II*. New York: Oxford University Press, 1991, p. 470.

6. John E. Findling and Frank W. Thackeray, eds., *Events That Changed America in the Twentieth Century*. Westport, CT: Greenwood Press, 1996, p. 191.

7. Harold Evans, *The American Century*. New York: Alfred A. Knopf, 1998, p. 616.

8. Evans, *The American Century*, p. 617.

9. U.S. Joint Congressional Committee on Inaugural Ceremonies, *Inaugural Addresses of the Presidents of the United States: From George Washington 1789 to George Bush 1989*. Washington, DC: Government Printing Office, 1989. www.cc.columbia.edu/acis/bartleby/inaugural/index.html.

10. Chafe, *The Unfinished Journey*, p. 474.

11. Quoted in Chafe, *The Unfinished Journey*, p. 465.

12. Quoted in Stuart A. Kallen, *A Cultural History of America Through the Decades: The 1980s*. San Diego: Lucent Books, 1999, p. 21.

13. Morgan and Wynn, *America's Century*, p. 200.

14. Quoted in Kallen, *A Cultural History of America Through the Decades: The 1980s*, p. 52.

15. Findling and Thackeray, *Events That Changed America in the Twentieth Century*, p. 196.

16. John Robson, "The Reagan Revolution: Interpretive Essay," in Findling and Thackeray, *Events That Changed America in the Twentieth Century*, p. 200.

17. Walter LaFeber, *America, Russia, and the Cold War, 1945–1996*. New York: McGraw Hill, 1997, p. 300.

18. Chafe, *The Unfinished Journey*, p. 491.

19. Joseph Smith, *The Cold War*. Malden, MA: Blackwell, 1998, p. 99.

20. Peter B. Levy, *Encyclopedia of the Reagan-Bush Years*. Westport, CT: Greenwood Press, 1996, p. 303.

21. LaFeber, *America, Russia, and the Cold War, 1945–1996*, p. 303.

22. Smith, *The Cold War*, p. 133.

23. Don Oberdorfer, *From the Cold War to a New Era: The United States and the Soviet Union, 1983–1991*. Baltimore: Johns Hopkins University Press, 1998, p. 107.

24. John Lewis Gaddis, *The United States and the End of the Cold War: Implications, Reconsiderations, Provocations*. New York: Oxford University Press, 1992.

25. Smith, *The Cold War*, p. 141.

26. Martin Walker, *The Cold War: A History*. New York: Henry Holt, 1993, p. 311.

27. Gale Stokes, *The Walls Came Tumbling Down: The Collapse of Communism in Eastern Europe*. New York: Oxford University Press, 1993, p. 141.

28. Quoted in Walker, *The Cold War*, p. 311.

29. Morgan and Wynn, *America's Century*, p. 208.

30. Alvin and Virginia Silverstein, *AIDS: Deadly Threat*. Hillside, NJ: Enslow, 1986, p. 7.

31. Mirko D. Grmek, *History of AIDS: Emergence and Origin of a Modern Pandemic*. Princeton, NJ: Princeton University Press, 1990, p. 40.

32. Myron A. Marty, *Daily Life in the United States, 1960–1990: Decades of Discord*. Westport, CT: Greenwood Press, 1997, p. 299.

33. Linda K. Fuller, *The Cosby Show: Audiences, Impact, and Implications*. Westport, CT: Greenwood Press, 1992, p. 17.

34. Quoted in Louis Giannetti and Scott Eyman, *Flashback: A Brief History of Film*. Englewood Cliffs, NJ: Prentice-Hall, 1996, p. 463.

35. William F. Palmer, *The Films of the Eighties: A Social History*. Carbondale and Edwardsville: Southern Illinois University Press, 1991, p. 208.

36. Giannetti and Eyman, *Flashback*, p. 464.

37. David Brode, *The Movies of the Eighties*. New York: Carol Publishing Group, 1990, p. 9.

CHAPTER 1

The Reagan Revolution

AMERICA'S DECADES

The Origins of '80s Conservatism

Iwan W. Morgan

Ronald Reagan's victory in the 1980 presidential election was due in large part to the unpopularity of his opponent and predecessor, Jimmy Carter. Despite some successes, the final year of Carter's administration was plagued with many problems, including economic recession, the Soviet invasion of Afghanistan, and the Iranian hostage crisis. By the summer of 1979 some public opinion polls ranked the Democrat as the most unpopular president in U.S. history. As Iwan W. Morgan explains, these were ideal circumstances for the New Right, the conservative wing of the Republican Party that supported Reagan's candidacy. Morgan is a professor of politics and government at the City of London Polytechnic, and the coeditor of *America's Century: Perspectives on U.S. History Since 1900*, from which the following essay is excerpted.

Jimmy Carter, an agribusinessman, born-again Christian, and former governor of Georgia, emerged from relative obscurity to win the 1976 presidential election. Owing to Watergate, Carter's status as an outsider and his promise that he would never lie to the American people were his main attractions. His banner issue was his pledge to curb the "imperial presidency," which he largely fulfilled. In many ways, however, Carter's presidency epitomized the age of un-

Excerpted from "The Age of Uncertainty," by Iwan W. Morgan in *America's Century: Perspectives on U.S. History Since 1900*, edited by Iwan W. Morgan and Neil A. Wynn. Copyright ©1993 by Holmes & Meier Publishers, Inc. Reprinted with permission from the publisher.

certainty, lacking as it did the kind of unifying theme and sense of direction that had characterized previous Democratic administrations. He never associated his name with a popular reform slogan, breaking a Democratic tradition that ran from Woodrow Wilson's New Freedom to Johnson's Great Society. His political values seemed rooted in contradiction. A liberal on social issues, Carter promised to fight for the underprivileged, but he also wanted to reduce federal expenditure and balance the budget by 1980. Reconciling these aims proved impossible, and in practice his fiscal conservatism prevailed. The aura of confusion permeating the Carter era was compounded by the post-Watergate context of American politics. Congress was in no mood to be compliant to the new president, who also lacked the political skills to save some of his major programs from defeat.

An Unpopular President

Scholarly opinion initially rated Carter an abject failure as president, but a revisionist view now suggests that he has been underestimated. Political scientist Erwin Hargrove depicts Carter as the legatee of southern Progressivism, for whom good government was based on expertise rather than popular politics, morality rather than power, public goods rather than particularist interests.[1] These values constituted both the strength and weakness of his presidency. Carter's outlook enabled him to break away from the conventional New Deal agenda and respond to the new issues of the late twentieth century, such as energy conservation, environmentalism, and tax reform. A willingness to innovate underlay his main domestic and international achievements, and his leadership gave the Democratic party a centrist image more in tune with the current political climate than traditional liberalism. Nevertheless, Carter's personal philosophy, which eschewed political horse-trading and accommodation of interest groups, ensured a stormy relationship with his party in Congress. Similarly, it prevented him from developing and appealing to the kind of popular constituency that had sustained his Democratic predecessors. When unmanageable problems, which were more the result of bad luck than misjudgment, blighted the final year of his presidency, he had no reservoir of public and political support to cushion him from the effects of economic and international failures.

Economy, efficiency, and equity in government were Carter's main domestic concerns. In line with his promise to restore fiscal integrity, he abandoned the "full-employment budget," initiated by Kennedy, in favor of the traditional method of calculating public finances. Convinced that the welfare system was unfair and wasteful, Carter proposed to amalgamate various income-transfer programs under a single budget, in order to target antipoverty spending more effectively without increasing the costs. This fell foul of Congress, where conservatives wanted expenditure cuts and liberals the opposite. To improve policy-making and administration in two crucial areas of modern government, Carter created new cabinet-level departments of Education and Energy. Major civil-service reforms that provided reward for merit were also implemented. To encourage domestic energy production, Carter decontrolled oil and natural-gas prices, but this was only enacted after an eighteen-month tussle with Congress. Adjunct proposals for a crude-oil tax, intended to encourage energy conservation and to finance energy grants for low-income families, and a windfall-profits tax on oil companies were lost because legislators responded to special-interest lobbies. To encourage competition, Carter also deregulated the airline, trucking, and railroad industries. Major environmental reforms met the requirements of equity and efficiency, and included controls over strip-mining, a superfund for chemical waste cleanup, and the establishment of the Arctic National Wilderness Reserve, which protected 100 million acres of Alaska from development and oil drilling.

Economic Recession and Gas Shortages

Carter's greatest domestic problem remained the economy. Recovery from the "Ford recession" had brought a new inflationary cycle whose effects were compounded by the credit explosion of the mid-1970s, when many Americans had taken advantage of the fact that interest rates were not climbing as rapidly as prices. Between 1974 and 1979 total business and household borrowing soared from $94 billion to $328 billion. Credit-card usage also became universal in this period, with the number of MasterCard holders alone leaping from 32 million to 57 million.

To correct this situation, Carter cut domestic program expenditure in 1979–80 and the Federal Reserve introduced draconian tight-money measures that sent the prime lending rate skyrocketing to an unprecedented 20 percent. Business retrenchment inevitably followed, with the automobile and construction industries suffering most. Already reeling from foreign competition, the giant Chrysler Corporation headed for bankruptcy until it was bailed out in 1980 by federal loan guarantees of $1.5 billion, made partly conditional on employees taking salary cuts. Economic recession depressed tax revenues, destroying Carter's hopes of balancing the budget, but rising unemployment was not accompanied by reduced inflation. Loan repayments became dearer and price decontrol pushed up energy costs. To make matters worse, a new revolutionary government in Iran cut off oil supplies to the United States, a close ally of the deposed shah. OPEC exploited this opportunity to raise its prices, which helped to double the cost of crude oil in 1979. With the discomfort index (inflation and unemployment) approaching a record 20 percent in 1980, many Americans judged Carter's economic policies a hopeless failure.

The Iranian Hostage Crisis and Other Foreign Policy Problems

Meanwhile, Carter's early foreign policy successes were overshadowed by crushing reverses during his final fifteen months in office. Voicing the national sense of decline, the journal *Business Week* lamented in 1980: "For the first time in its history, the United States is no longer growing in power and influence among the nations of the world."[2]

The post–Vietnam War challenge facing the United States was to exercise world leadership without hegemony. In addressing this, Carter manifested a Wilsonian emphasis on international cooperation and peace. His greatest tri-

Christian Fundamentalism and the Moral Majority

The New Right's concern with restoring moral order found support among fundamentalist Christian sects. They expressed outrage over the greater acceptance of divorce, abortion, pre-marital sex, homosexuality, and feminism. . . .

In the decade following 1978, the number of Christian ministries broadcast regularly over television increased from twenty-five to over three hundred. Evangelical Christians carried out a communications revolution. They and Reagan embraced each other, increasing their mutual power throughout the 1980s.

Jerry Falwell, a minister in Virginia, proclaimed that "this country is fed up with radical causes . . . fed up with the unisex movement, fed up with the departure from basics, from decency, from the philosophy of the monogamous home." The free enterprise system, he insisted, "is clearly outlined in the Book of Proverbs." In 1979 Falwell created a political arm of fundamentalism, called the Moral Majority, which sought to arouse evangelical Protestants, to "get them saved, baptized and registered" to vote. . . .

Falwell and several other ministers, including Pat Robertson, Jimmy Swaggert, Oral Roberts, and Jim Bakker became especially adept at preaching the gospel on television. By 1980, these so-called Televangelists had a weekly audience estimated at between 60 to 100 million viewers. These electronic ministries combined country music, sermons, and support for conservative causes with an extraordinarily sophisticated fund-raising apparatus.

Michael Schaller, *Reckoning with Reagan: America and Its President in the 1980s.* New York: Oxford University Press, 1992.

umph was in personally negotiating the Camp David Accords of 1978, which laid the foundation for an Egyptian-Israeli peace treaty. While this left the Palestinian problem unresolved and did not include Syria, it still stands as the most significant contribution to the search for peace in the Middle East. Carter's efforts to increase U.S. moral influence in the Third World also marked a departure from Cold War traditions. Some attempt was made, albeit with limited success, to pressure Latin American dictatorships into better observance of human rights, support for racist regimes in Namibia and Zimbabwe was terminated, and following a tough battle for Senate ratification, a treaty scheduled the Panama Canal's restoration to native control in the year 2000. Also, though more from indecision than idealism, the Carter administration eschewed intervention when pro-U.S. dictatorships in Iran and Nicaragua were threatened by revolution and finally overthrown.

Nevertheless, Carter was too bound by recent orthodoxy to establish truly new foundations for U.S. foreign policy. The Cold War was reinvigorated following the Soviet invasion of Afghanistan in 1979. Already weakened by a renewed arms race, superpower rivalry in Africa, and Carter's criticism of Soviet human rights, détente was now in ruins. Some analysts, like George F. Kennan, considered the Soviets' action a defensive measure against the spread of Islamic fundamentalism along their southern borders, but the administration saw it as an expansionist threat to Western oil supplies. The Carter Doctrine proclaimed that the United States would intervene, militarily and unilaterally if necessary, to prevent further Soviet advances toward the Persian Gulf. In addition, Carter announced a defense program designed to restore U.S. military superiority, signifying what historian Gaddis Smith called a "return to militarism."[3] In reality, the roots of Ronald Reagan's defense buildup lay in Carter's military budgets, which sanctioned the largest new weapons programs in nearly thirty years.

This response did not dispel the popular conviction that Carter had allowed American power to decline to unacceptable levels. His failure to compel Soviet withdrawal from Afghanistan and OPEC's continued excess were viewed as evidence of U.S. weakness. The most humiliating episode of all was the Iranian hostage crisis. In November 1979, militants seized the U.S. embassy in Tehran and held its personnel hostage for 444 days, in an effort to force Carter to send home for trial the deposed shah (who was in New York for medical treatment) and apologize for past U.S. involvement in Iran. Moral suasion, economic pressure, and an abortive military rescue mission failed to secure the hostages' release. The crisis left Americans yearning for a leader who would restore their power and prestige in world affairs.

Reagan's Landslide Victory in 1980

The problems that engulfed Carter at home and abroad resulted in his landslide defeat in the 1980 election by Ronald Reagan, whose coattails also produced the first GOP Senate majority since 1952 and substantially increased Republican strength in the House. Conservatives viewed the election as a turning point similar to that of 1932 and anticipated that Reagan would be the "Roosevelt of the Right." Liberalism, the fount of new ideas throughout the twentieth century, had run out of intellectual steam in the face of America's economic and international decline. In contrast, the U.S. Right, like its counterpart in Britain under Margaret Thatcher, had rediscovered its intellectual vigor in the late 1970s and transformed itself from a reactionary into an innovative force. Appalled by the results of diplomacy and conciliation, conservatives were adamant that American interests abroad could only be protected by an expansion of military power. They were also in fundamental agreement that less government involvement in the economy was the road to salvation.

Many conservatives wanted deep cuts in the welfare state to balance the budget and finance tax reduction. Grassroots support for this view was manifest in 1978 when California voters approved the Proposition 13 referendum to reduce property taxes and put stringent limits on state expenditure for social programs. Others on the right wanted to go much further than Jimmy Carter had done in rolling back the regulatory state, which they considered a drag on the competitiveness of American business. Finally, and most importantly, supply-side economics gained respectability in place of neo-Keynesian doctrines, first among segments of the academic community, and then with Republicans like Congressmen Jack Kemp of New York and David Stockman of Michigan. This theory bore some resemblance to the trickle-down economics popular in the 1920s, but the supply-siders believed that tax cuts should precede a balanced budget. Their game plan also envisaged expenditure cuts across the board rather than in selected programs, though it did accept the necessity for a welfare safety net for the poor. The essence of supply-side doctrine was that tax cuts for corporations and high earners would boost investment, thereby reviving the economy to the benefit of all groups in society. Prosperity would also bring greater tax revenues for government, thus eliminating the budget deficit in conjunction with expenditure reductions.

The Christian Right

The conservative resurgence also drew strength from the growth of religious fundamentalism. In the late 1970s the Christian Right began to flex its muscles against the forces of modernism, demanding a reassertion of traditional values and behavior. With crusading zeal, it initially attacked the sociocultural legacies of the 1960s, notably feminism, the permissive society, and secularism. Unlike previous outbursts of fundamentalist protest such as that of the 1920s, however, the new movement made no distinction between moral and political issues. The Christian Right stood for the conservative rebirth of the nation and its government. A healthy economy was deemed a moral imperative, for which lower federal expenditures and a balanced budget were essential prerequisites. Fundamentalists were equally adamant that higher defense spending was a vital antidote to the international expansion of godless communism.

New organizational and technological developments enabled the modern Right to propagandize its messages very effectively. A host of conservative interest groups sprang up in the 1970s, the most famous being the National Conservative Political Action Committee, an ideological organization whose activities in the 1980 election helped to defeat prominent liberal senators, and the Moral Majority, which had over two million members and articulated the political aims of the Christian Right. These organizations, small and large, reached out to the grass roots and acquired substantial funding through the new techniques of computerized mailing lists. Cable television development also led to the establishment of religious broadcast networks, through which TV evangelists, like Pat Robertson, could preach to a total audience of some thirty million.

Contrasting Views of the "Reagan Revolution"

The standard-bearer of the New Right, Ronald Reagan, a former Hollywood actor and two-term governor of California, became the most popular president of recent times. A master communicator, he articulated conservative goals in a manner that appealed to a wide audience, and his engaging style and supreme optimism helped to restore national self-confidence. On the other hand, Reagan was no master of detail and sought only to shape the general direction of his administration's programs. Aides and cabinet department heads assumed responsibility for detailed policy-making. The shortcomings of this system of delegation were revealed by the Iran-Contra affair, an illegal arms-for-hostages deal that National Security Council officials apparently arranged without the president's knowledge. Critical of Reagan's hands-off leadership style, some observers, particularly foreign analysts, saw him as a bumbling incompetent, whose popularity was the result of skillful public relations rather than substantive achievement. By contrast, British political scientist David Mervin adjudges Reagan the most effective president since Roosevelt, in terms of his success in changing the course of public policy, his legacy as party leader, and his revitalization of the presidency.[4] This assessment is certainly closer to the truth than the highly negative view of Reagan, but it is important not to exaggerate the extent and success of the "Reagan Revolution."

1. Erwin C. Hargrove, *Jimmy Carter as President: Leadership and the Politics of the Public Good* (Baton Rouge, La., 1988), especially pp. 6–32.

2. Quoted in Walter LaFeber, *The American Age: United States Foreign Policy at Home and Abroad Since 1750* (New York, 1989), p. 666.

3. Gaddis Smith, *Morality, Reason, and Power: American Diplomacy in the Carter Years* (New York, 1986), p. 9.

4. David Mervin, *Ronald Reagan and the Presidency* (New York, 1990), especially pp. 1–11, 175–222. See also his article "Ronald Reagan's Place in History," *Journal of American Studies* 23 (1989): 269–86.

Reagan's Policies Shape American Politics

George Moss

One of Ronald Reagan's most famous quotes is "Government is not the solution to our problems; government is the problem." This statement succinctly summarizes both his and the New Right's political philosophy. The Reagan administration favored reducing taxes and lowering spending on programs such as welfare and school lunches. In advocating a turn away from government, Reagan became the first president to openly oppose policies of the New Deal, the name given to the large number of government programs implemented under Franklin D. Roosevelt in the 1930s to help people recover from the Great Depression. However, as historian George Moss explains in this excerpt from his book *America in the Twentieth Century*, Reagan did not oppose Social Security and Medicare—the most popular and expensive social programs—and he also significantly increased spending on the military. Thus taxes decreased while spending did not, and America's budget deficit reached record levels during the Reagan years.

T wo weeks shy of his seventieth birthday at the time of his inauguration, Ronald Reagan was the oldest man ever to become President. . . .

Reaganomics

When Reagan took office in January 1981, runaway inflation had ravaged the American economy for years. The average family's purchasing power was about $1,000 less than it had been a decade earlier. The value of the dollar had declined by 50 percent in five years. The new President called upon his fellow Americans to join him "in a new beginning" to clean up "the worst economic mess since the Great Depression." He blamed "the mess" on high levels of government spending and taxation. He said, "Government is not the solution to our problems; government is the problem."

President Reagan grounded his program for economic recovery in "supply-side" economic theory. Contradicting the long-prevailing Keynesian theory, which relied on government spending and tax cuts to boost consumer demand, supply-siders favored cutting both federal spending and taxes at the same time. They believed that the private sector, freed from shackles imposed by government spending and high taxes, would increase its investment in productive enterprises, and this would generate economic growth and create millions of new jobs. Such expansion would also cut inflation and generate tax revenues that would more than offset losses from the reduced tax rates. The expansion would also balance the budget. To many skeptics, "Reaganomics" sounded almost too good to be true.

The President brought a mixed group of economic advisers to Washington. At the Treasury Department, he installed Donald Regan, a Wall Street securities broker and a conventional conservative Republican. David Stockman became Director of the Office of Management and Budget. Stockman, a supply-side zealot, carried Reagan's program of cutting spending and reducing taxes to Congress. A brilliant workaholic and a missionary for cost and tax cuts, Stockman mastered the intricacies of the congressional budgetary process. He was the point-man for Reaganomics. While Stockman overhauled the federal budgetary process, Paul Volcker, a Carter holdover and chairman of the Federal Reserve Board, kept tight reins on the money supply.

Stockman made cutting federal spending the Reagan administration's top priority. He slashed $41 billion in social spending for food stamps, public service jobs, student loans, school lunches, urban mass transit, and welfare payments. Middle-class entitlements, such as Social Security, were exempted and Reagan also left what he called a "safety net for the truly needy." At the same time he was cutting back social spending, Reagan also significantly increased military spending. The President exhibited great political skill and powers of persuasion by convincing many Sunbelt Democratic congressmen to support his programs. These "boll weevils," led by Representative Phil Gramm of Texas, were crucial to getting his program through the Democratic-controlled House. Reagan made a dramatic personal appearance before a joint session of Congress to plead for his budget only a few weeks after being seriously wounded during an assassin's attempt on his life. He built up a strong bipartisan coalition in the House and won a commanding 253 to 176 vote victory. His winning margin in the Senate was even more impressive, 78 to 20. Liberal Democrats were skeptical that supply-side economics could work as its disciples insisted it must, but they lacked an alternative program that commanded public support.

Limiting the Role of Government

The President also succeeded in getting his proposed income tax cuts through. He originally called for cuts of 10 percent per year for three years, but accepted a compromise proposal that cut taxes 5 percent the first year and then 10 percent for the next two years. The House accepted the 25 percent tax cuts and the Senate approved them overwhelmingly. Several other tax concessions were written into an omnibus bill. Capital gains, inheritance tax, and gift taxes were also reduced. Business tax write-offs were also enhanced.

Reagan also sought to achieve his goal of restricting government activity and reducing federal regulation of the economy. He appointed men and women to federal regulatory agencies who shared his views that markets, not government agencies, ought to direct the national economy. His most controversial appointment was James Watt to head the Department of the Interior. Watt was a conservative ideologue who headed an antienvironmentalist legal action group before his appointment to the Interior Department. He supported strip-mining and opening up public lands to private developers, including offshore oil-drilling sites.

Drew Lewis, Reagan's Secretary of Transportation, removed many of the regulations to reduce pollution and to increase driver safety that had been imposed on the U.S. auto industry during the 1970s. He also persuaded the Japanese to voluntarily restrict automobile imports to the United States. Lewis opposed an illegal strike by an air traffic controller's union (PATCO) in the summer of 1981. President Reagan fired the striking workers, decertified the union, and ordered Lewis to train and hire thousands of new air controllers to replace them. . . .

Recession and Recovery

After a year, it was evident that Reaganomics had not brought the promised economic revival. In January 1982, unemployment exceeded 9 percent, the highest since 1941. Business bankruptcies rose to depression levels. Steep interest rates priced homes and cars beyond the reach of millions of families and plunged those two major industries into depression. One year after Reagan's promised new beginning, the nation was mired in its worst slump since the Great Depression. Big cities fared the worst. In Detroit, unemployment reached 20 percent. A class of "new poor," not seen since the 1930s, appeared on the streets: homeless, unemployed workers and their families. . . .

The economy recovered strongly in 1983 and 1984. The gross national product rose 6.8 percent in 1984, the largest one year gain since the Korean War. Unemployment and interest rates declined. Housing starts and new car sales picked up; domestic auto makers reported strong sales and record profits in mid-1984. The rate of inflation dropped to 4 percent for both years, the lowest since the early 1970s. Abundant world oil supplies were an important cause of the drop in the rate of inflation. By the end of 1984, the OPEC cartel was in disarray and world oil prices were falling.

All economic news was not good, however. Tax cuts combined with large increases in military spending to generate record federal deficits—$195 billion in 1983 and $175 billion in 1984. By the end of his first term, President Reagan had managed to double the national debt. All talk of balanced budgets had been replaced by a frenzied concern to staunch the flow of red ink. Over 7.5 million Americans remained out of work. The Census Bureau reported the nation's poverty rate reached 15.2 percent in 1983, the highest since 1965. A 15.2 percent poverty rate meant that there were 35 million poor people in America, 6 million more than when Reagan assumed office. . . .

Reagan's Second Term

Two serious economic problems continued to plague Reagan's second administration. Budget deficits continued to grow, exceeding $200 billion in 1986. Trade deficits also had expanded rapidly between 1980 and 1985 as imports increased 41 percent while exports decreased slightly. In December 1985, Congress enacted a measure that required automatic annual reductions in the budget deficit if the President and Congress failed to agree on cuts. The following year, the Supreme Court nullified the law and the deficit for 1986 came in at a record $226 billion. The 1987 deficit was somewhat smaller, but it took a record crash of the stock market on October 19, 1987 and fears of impending recession, to force Reagan and the Congress to reduce the budget deficit. They were forced to come up with a combination of proposed spending cuts and tax increases amounting to $76 billion over two years, a politically painful dose of fiscal medicine for both Republicans and Democrats.

During his second term, President Reagan continued to appoint conservative jurists to the federal bench. The Administration searched for strict constructionists whose constitutional views could also incorporate right-wing social agendas, including opposition to affirmative action programs, abortion, and pornography. Reaganite judges were also expected to support efforts to restore prayer in the public schools and to favor the death penalty,

The President also had opportunities to reshape the Supreme Court. In 1981 he had appointed Sandra Day O'Connor and in 1986 he had selected Antonin Scalia to be associate justices. Both O'Connor and Scalia were conservatives. Reagan had also replaced retiring Chief Justice Warren Burger with Associate Justice William Rehnquist, the most conservative member of the Court. Reagan's efforts to add a third justice to the High Court in the fall of 1987 proved embarrassing to the elderly chief executive. His first nominee, Appellate Judge Robert Bork, was rejected by the Senate because of his extreme views concerning First Amendment rights. Reagan's second choice, Douglas Ginsburg, was forced to withdraw his name from consideration after revealing to the press that he had smoked marijuana when a student and also while teaching

© Harley Schwadron. Reprinted with permission.

at Harvard Law School. Reagan's third choice, also a judicial conservative, Anthony Kennedy, a popular choice, was unanimously confirmed by the Senate in February 1988. Even with the Reagan appointments aboard, however, Supreme Court decisions continued to reflect a moderate, non-ideological pattern. In a 1986 decision, the Court reaffirmed women's rights to get abortions; a 1987 decision upheld the principle of affirmative action. . . .

Toward the 1990s

As the 1980s wound down, the American economy continued to perform strongly. The economy shrugged off the effects of the October 19, 1987 stock market crash, the worst one-day selling panic in American financial history. Alarmists had feared that the 22.6 percent drop in equity values that occurred that day would trigger a recession or even depression as had happened in 1929. But six months after the 1987 Crash, the gross national product was growing at a rate of 4 percent per year and unemployment stood at 5.6 percent, the lowest in a decade. One hundred fourteen million Americans, the most ever, were working and the economy continued to generate thousands of new jobs each month. Inflation remained in check. The expansionist trend that had begun in 1983 continued. An important reason for the economy's strong performance following the 1987 stock market collapse was that, under the leadership of Alan Greenspan, the Federal Reserve quickly expanded the money supply and lowered interest rates. In 1929, officials at the Fed had allowed the money supply to contract following the Great Crash, helping to drive the economy into depression.

Even though the U.S. economy continued to perform strongly, there were some trouble signs. American exports were not expanding, and many sectors of the farm economy remained weak. The dollar continued to decline in value relative to other strong national currencies such as the Japanese yen and the West German Deutschmark. Continuing large budget and trade deficits, and the unresolved debt problems of Third World nations, remained clouds on the U.S. economic horizon.

As the 1980s approached their end, so did the Reagan presidency. During his final two years of office he lacked the popularity and power that he had enjoyed during the first six years of his presidency. He had been badly wounded politically by Iranscam and continual revelations of other wrongdoings by current and former high officials in his administration. He was forced to compromise his policies and programs with a resurgent Democratically-controlled Congress.

The Truth About the 1980s Economy

Michael Schaller

Conservatives often contend that the 1980s was a period of great economic prosperity, while critics of Reagan argue that his policies led to the rich getting richer and the poor getting poorer. In the following excerpt from his book *Reckoning with Reagan: America and Its President in the 1980s,* University of Arizona history professor Michael Schaller explains that there is some truth to both claims. The economy did rebound quickly after a slump in 1982, and in the mid-80s a series of corporate mergers, insider trading scandals, and the emergence of "yuppies" all seemed to point to people's growing obsession with wealth. But by the end of the decade it was clear that some groups were worse off than they had been in the 1970s. Moreover, Schaller notes that the effects of "Reaganomics" on all these trends is still a topic of debate.

R onald Reagan had an impact on American government and society that was both less than he claimed and greater than his critics admitted. The president took credit for what he called the longest post-1945 period of economic growth, a reduction in the size, cost, and scope of government, a rebirth of national spirit, and the restoration of "traditional" values in such varied spheres as judicial de-

---

cision making and private moral behavior. Administration policies affected all this and more, although not always in ways Reagan understood. . . .

The National Debt

In his first economic message as president, Reagan blamed the Democrats for mortgaging the future to finance current consumption. By the mid-1980s, Democratic politicians and many economists charged that Reagan had placed the federal government on the equivalent of a credit-card buying binge. Instead of "tax and spend liberals," "borrow and spend conservatives," dominated government.

Both the government and private industry thrived on unprecedented levels of indebtedness. During Reagan's two terms the cumulative national debt tripled, from about $900 billion to almost $2.7 trillion. Interest payments alone cost taxpayers $200 billion per year. Government borrowing absorbed three-fourths of the annual net savings of families and businesses. In light of this, some cynics labeled Reagan's talk of balanced budgets a "classic case of a drunk preaching temperance."

The domestic borrowing pool had to be supplemented by large infusions of foreign capital, especially from Japan and Germany. By the late-1980s, foreign investors held as much as 20% of the national debt. In less than a decade, the United States went from being the world's biggest creditor to the world's biggest debtor. Instead of interest payments on the debt flowing into private American coffers, a growing portion of the payments flowed out of the country.

The nation's foreign trade deficit also grew dramatically during the 1980s. Near the start of the decade, the value of foreign manufactured imports surpassed by about $26 billion the value of American manufactured products sold abroad. By the end of the decade, the United States ran a deficit of more than $150 billion per year. Every week, on average during the 1980s, American consumers spent about $2 billion more abroad than foreigners spent on American products. The cumulative trade imbalance for the decade approached $1 trillion.

Foreign investors used their dollar surpluses to buy American real estate, factories, and stock shares. Some economists considered this a healthy vote of confidence. Foreign investments provided jobs for Americans. But business profits—and decision-making power—flowed abroad. Economic security depended increasingly on Japanese, British, German, Dutch, and Saudi willingness to buy the public and private debt of the United States. . . .

The Culture of Greed

Supply-siders certainly achieved their goal of reversing New Deal style income redistribution programs. Not only did resources cease to flow from wealthier to less well off Americans, but a substantial portion of national wealth was redistributed to Germany and Japan. Reagan-era policies practically doubled the share of national income going to the wealthiest 1% of Americans, from 8.1 to about 15%. In 1980, 4,400 individuals filed income tax returns reporting an adjusted gross income of over $1 million. By 1987, over 35,000 taxpayers filed such returns. The net worth of the 400 richest Americans nearly tripled. In 1980 a typical corporate chief executive officer (CEO) made about 40 times the income of an average factory worker, nine years later the CEO made 93 times as much. Lawyers handling business mergers also gained great wealth. Over 1,300 partners of major law firms averaged higher pay than the 800 top executives in industry.

Not since the Gilded Age of the late nineteenth century or the Roaring Twenties had the acquisition and flaunting of wealth been so publicly celebrated as during the 1980s. Income became the accepted measure of one's value to society. Professional athletes earned immense sums as teams scrambled to recruit basketball, football, and baseball players from colleges. Congressman Kemp, economist Laffer, and writers Jude Wanniski and George Gilder celebrated financiers and deal makers as secular saints, enriching society. In his bestselling book *Wealth and Poverty*

(1981) and opinion pieces appearing in the *Wall Street Journal,* Gilder emerged as a theologian of capitalism. "Faith in man, faith in the future, faith in the rising returns of giving, faith in the mutual benefits of trade, faith in the providence of God are all essential to successful capitalism," he wrote. In the gospel according to Gilder, "Capitalism begins with giving . . . thus the contest of gifts leads to an expansion of human sympathies." Accumulating wealth represented the highest morality. Only the unsuccessful blamed the system for their problems. The poor of the 1980s, he claimed, "are refusing to work hard."

Gilder, Laffer, and Wanniski identified the true heroes of the age as Wall Street operators such as Carl Icahn, T. Boone Pickens, Ivan Boesky, and Michael Milken and real estate speculator Donald Trump—men who earned billions of dollars buying and merging companies and in construction. They were celebrated as role models and builders of a better world.

Merger Mania, Junk Bonds, and Insider Trading

A "merger mania," fueled by changes in the 1981 tax law and a relaxed attitude toward enforcement of anti-trust statutes by the Reagan Justice Department, gripped Wall Street through 1987. Boesky and Milken exemplified the "risk arbitrageur," financiers who discovered ways to make fortunes by borrowing money to merge and acquire large enterprises. Many of the nation's biggest companies bought up competitors or were themselves swallowed up in leveraged buyouts, financed by huge loans bearing high interest rates. Corporate raiders argued that these deals rewarded stockholders and got rid of incompetent management, thus increasing competitiveness.

Because many multi-billion dollar deals were too risky for banks, insurance, or pension funds to finance, Milken and others pioneered the use of "junk bonds." Corporate raiders issued these I.O.U.s that paid very high rates of interest. Repayment of the heavy debt often compelled the purchaser to sell off or "strip" portions of the newly acquired business.

Many of the nation's largest corporations, including R.J. Reynolds, Nabisco, Walt Disney, Gulf, Federated Department Stores, and R.H. Macy were the objects of leveraged buyouts, some willingly and others under protest. Between 1984 and 1987, twenty-one mergers valued at over $1 billion each occurred. Many corporations sought to avoid hostile takeovers by boosting immediate profitability to stockholders by going heavily into debt through issuing bonds or paying special dividends. This increased indebtedness made a buyout more expensive and less attractive to outsiders. It left the company less able to raise funds for investment in plants and new products.

Costly mergers did not necessarily or even usually produce a more competitive company. But immense profits were earned through arranging financing of the takeover, issuing junk bonds, or acting as a consultant to the deal. For example, in 1987 Michael Milken earned an estimated $550 million in fees. By age 40, he had become a billionaire.

Critics of these activities charged that money spent on acquisitions contributed nothing to the productive capacity of the economy since it did not go into research or new product lines. The debt incurred by mergers became a long-term burden. Corporate profits went mainly to paying bondholders, not investing in new plants. In any period of recession, when profits dipped, it seemed likely that leveraged corporations would have difficulty paying interest on the costly junk bonds. . . .

The junk bond market shrank dramatically by 1988, especially as heavily indebted companies began to default on payments and go into bankruptcy.

Yuppies

In mid-decade, a new social category emerged on the American scene. *Newsweek* magazine called 1984 "The Year of the Yuppie," an acronym for young, urban, upwardly mobile professionals. For a time, this group seemed as charmed as the Wall Street wizards. *Newsweek*, in particular, applauded the group's eagerness to "go for it" as a sign of the "yuppie virtues of imagination, daring and entrepreneurship." Yuppies existed "on a new plane of consciousness, a state of Transcendental Acquisition."

Demographers and advertisers first used the term. Journalists popularized it in 1983–84, partly to explain Senator Gary Hart's unexpected popularity among young Americans as he campaigned for the Democratic presidential nomination. Unlike radical protesters or hippies of the 1960s, these young adults were hardly social rebels. They plunged joyously into the American mainstream ready to consume.

Certified yuppies—people born between 1945 and 1959, earning over $40,000 as a professional or manager, and living in a city—totaled about 1.5 million. As candidate Hart learned, they were not a reliable constituency for Democratic liberals. Yuppies tended to be "pro-choice" on the abortion issue, enjoyed "recreational drugs," and supported Reagan's economic policies. They aspired to become investment bankers, not social workers. In 1985, for example, one-third of the entire senior class at Yale sought jobs as financial analysts at First Boston Corporation.

Yuppies enjoyed creature comforts, indulging themselves, when possible, with "leisure products" like Porsches and BMWs, expensive sneakers, state-of-the-art electronic equipment, and gourmet foods. They flocked to health spas, wore designer clothes made of natural fibers, jogged, and put a high value on "looking good.". . .

The Wall Street Crash of October 19, 1987, ended the mystique surrounding young entrepreneurs. That day, as the dimension of the collapse expanded, anxious crowds gathered outside the New York Stock Exchange. A man began shouting, "The end is near! It's all over! The Reagan Revolution is over! Down with MBAs! Down with Yuppies!" Another member of the crowd tried to bolster confidence by yelling, "Whoever dies with the most toys wins!"

After only four years of grace, the term yuppie evolved into a slur. In 1988 *Newsweek* declared the group in "disgrace" and even suggested that the '80s were over, two years early. The *Wall Street Journal* reported "conspicuous consumption is passé." *New York* magazine, a purveyor to yuppie tastes, ran a cover story celebrating altruism and asked its readers: "HAD IT WITH PRIDE, COVETOUSNESS, LUST, ANGER, GLUTTONY, ENVY AND SLOTH? IT'S TIME TO START DOING GOOD."

The Other Americans

Far less glamorous than either the risk arbitrageurs of Wall Street or the yuppies of Los Angeles were the people of average income and the poor. Their experience during the 1980s differed markedly from the fables of wealth told by George Gilder. Measured in constant dollars, the average family income of the poorest fifth of the population dropped (from $5,439 to $4,107) while the income of the richest fifth swelled from $62,000 to $69,000. During the Reagan Recovery, the most affluent fifth of American households experienced a 14% increase in their wealth while the middle three-fifths experienced little or no improvement. Put simply, the rich got richer and everyone else tread water.

As a justification of his tax policy, President Reagan maintained that despite the cut in tax rates after 1981, federal revenues had grown. He neglected to mention that they never increased enough to cover the large expansion in military expenditures. But his assertion obscured the fact that the rate reductions favored the wealthy and that the total tax bite (which included Social Security, state, and sales taxes) paid by the average American family did not diminish and even increased slightly during the 1980s.

Economic growth after 1983 seemed impressive when compared to the late 1970s, but appeared less so when the base of comparison became the period from the Second World War through the Carter administration. Overall, the economy grew at a faster rate during the 1960s and 1970s than in the 1980s. Unemployment remained higher during the 1980s than in most years from 1947 to 1973. Real wages, which began to stagnate during the 1970s, continued to do so. In aggregate, individual salaries declined slightly during the Reagan years. The impact of this, however, was hidden because of a substantial increase in the number of working wives and mothers who boosted total family income. By 1989, the wealthiest two-fifths of American families received 67.8% of national income, while the bottom two-fifths earned a mere 15.4%—a larger spread than at any time since 1945.

Women and children were the most likely to be poor. The number of children living in poverty, one in five, had grown by 24% during the 1980s. The so-called feminization of poverty also grew more severe during the Reagan decade. The percentage of children living with a never married mother more than doubled during the 1980s, from 2.9 to 7%. By 1989 one of every four births in the United States was to an unwed woman. African-American and Hispanic women had the highest likelihood of becoming single mothers. Unwed mothers were less likely to receive prenatal care, finish high school, or hold a paying job.

A Major Transformation in the Nature of Poverty

These problems had complex causes and Reagan's policies were by no means responsible for creating them. But the refusal of his administration to address them seriously made the situation worse. In a particularly counterproductive move, the Reagan administration slashed spending for the WIC (Women-Infants-Children) program that provided pre- and post-natal care to poor women and helped reduce infant mortality rates and future medical costs.

Reagan defended reductions in social welfare spending with a typical quip. America, he remarked, had fought a war on poverty for nearly twenty years before he took office "and poverty won." At first glance, statistics he quoted seemed to confirm his dismal assessment. After an initial decline in the poverty rate to about 13% during the late Johnson and early Nixon administrations, the rate stalled at this level through the early 1980s.

But these aggregate numbers masked a major transformation in the nature of poverty. Increased spending on programs such as Social Security and Medicare dramatically improved the lot of the elderly and handicapped. They were much less likely to be poor by the 1980s than at any time since 1945. The bulk of the poor after 1980 consisted of single mothers, young children, and young minority men with little education and few job skills. These groups had either not been the beneficiaries of anti-poverty programs during the 1970s or were left in the lurch by spending cuts in such programs.

Rather than welfare spending "causing" dependency, as many conservatives argued, the surging rates of teen pregnancy, the breakdown of stable family structures in the minority community, and the loss of millions of basic manufacturing jobs in cities, where most of the poor now lived, contributed to the creation of the "new poor.". . .

The Urban Underclass

Both conservatives and liberals were troubled by the increasing size of a permanent homeless population and a seemingly unreachable urban "underclass." The underclass consisted largely of minorities, especially African-Americans. The homeless were divided among women and children fleeing abusive spouses, unskilled individuals with social problems, and the chronically mentally ill. Many lived on city streets, in parks, or in subway stations, begging for money and food. Reagan dismissed the problem by suggesting homeless people were either nuts or people who enjoyed their lifestyle. While true in some cases, it vastly oversimplified the problem. The president showed no interest in boosting support for community mental health programs that might aid the chronic mentally ill.

The specter of the homeless and urban underclass unsettled American sensibilities but had little effect on public policy. Conservatives saw poverty primarily as a personal failure. Government efforts to help only made matters worse and provided a disincentive for individual effort. Liberals believed government had a responsibility to help, but offered few suggestions beyond restoring funds cut from social service programs.

The 1984 Election: The Height of Reagan's Popularity

William H. Chafe

Ronald Reagan has often been called the "Great Communicator" by his admirers, because of his remarkable ability to articulate his political ideals and beliefs. He has also been called the "Teflon president" (after the material used in nonstick cookware) by more critical observers, who note how easily Reagan was able to brush aside criticism of his policies. As William H. Chafe, author of *The Unfinished Journey: America Since World War II* explains, nothing illustrates Reagan's popularity better than the 1984 presidential election, in which Reagan defeated Walter Mondale, the Democrat who had served as vice president under Jimmy Carter. As Chafe notes, Reagan's popularity was due in large part to the fact that America's economy was booming in 1984, an advantage that would not last—but at the time, Reagan seemed politically invulnerable.

In another age and time, Walter Mondale might have been a sure bet to win the presidency. The son of a minister and piano teacher, descendant of Norwegian stock, and the anointed heir of Hubert Humphrey, Mondale embodied the midwestern ethos of hard work, compassion, and public service. His political career represented a lifetime of preparation for the nation's highest office. A student leader

Excerpted from *The Unfinished Journey: America Since WWII*, 3rd ed., by William H. Chafe. Copyright ©1986, 1991, 1995 by Oxford University Press, Inc. Reprinted with permission from Oxford University Press, Inc.

at Macalester College, he became Humphrey's protege as attorney general in Minnesota, then moved on to the U.S. Senate to carry forward the New Deal/New Frontier program of liberal democracy. Mondale was bright, he worked hard, and his colleagues respected him. After Jimmy Carter chose him as his running mate in 1976, Mondale became a full partner in the new administration, playing—with Carter's encouragement—an active and daily role in all major decisions. He knew the tensions, the ambiguities, the challenges of the Oval Office better than any person except the president himself. Mondale was ready.

Mondale's Campaign Strategy

In 1984 the Minnesotan also believed he could win—not easily, to be sure, but if Mondale could draw together the New Deal coalition, add a few allies, and appeal to America's sense of "fairness," maybe he could do it. After all, even Reagan's budget director, David Stockman, had admitted that the Reagan tax program was simply the old Herbert Hoover "trickle-down" theory revisited. If one gave enough to the rich, it would eventually have some impact on the poor. "I mean," Stockman told a reporter, "[our proposals were] always a Trojan Horse to bring down the top tax rates." The result, Yale University economist James Tobin noted, was the redistribution of "income, wealth and power—from government to private enterprise, from workers to capitalist, from poor to rich." Mondale believed that the country would reject this "class struggle on behalf of the rich."

With equal conviction, Mondale believed that voters favored a relaxation of world tensions. More than 70 percent of all Americans supported a nuclear freeze with the Soviet Union. Three-quarters of a million people had demonstrated in New York City on behalf of such a freeze. Reagan's arms build-up not only fueled out-of-control deficits, it also created the possibility of confrontation with the Soviet Union. As George Kennan wrote in 1983, Soviet-American relations were in a "dreadful and dangerous condition." Reagan's rhetoric, the father of containment wrote, was "childish, inexcusably childish, unworthy of a people charged with responsibility for conducting the affairs of a great power in an endangered world." Whether or not the average citizen would go that far, there seemed ample evidence from the polls that most Americans were deeply disturbed by the possibility of a new Vietnam in Central America and wished for a shift in Soviet-American relations from confrontation to cooperation.

With these concerns as a base, Mondale was convinced that he could put together a coalition that would successfully challenge the president. Political scientists had blamed Democratic failures in the 1970s on the party's inability to retain traditional Democratic constituencies. Now, Mondale sought out these constituencies, going to the AFL-CIO, the National Education Association, civil rights groups, and women's organizations for support. According to public opinion polls, the most significant new political phenomenon in America was the "gender gap." Women differed from men by 10 to 15 points when asked about war and peace, or social justice at home. If he could cultivate the support of groups like the National Organization for Women, go back to the trade unions, and sell his case on fairness at home and relaxation of tensions abroad—then, Mondale believed, he could line up the troops and begin a march to victory.

In this election year, however, even a good idea turned on itself. Critics charged that the former vice-president was *too* subservient to special interest groups. He seemed to *pander* to the unions, the teachers, the blacks. Moreover, he was dull, familiar, too predictable. And then there were the other pursuers of the prize—John Glenn, trying to be his party's answer to Reagan, an all-American hero whose life was about to be memorialized in a movie; Gary Hart, the young, attractive senator who talked about new ideas, looked like John Kennedy, chopped his right hand like Kennedy, fingered his coat button like Kennedy; Alan Cranston, the nuclear freeze candidate; and Jesse Jackson, the charismatic disciple of Martin Luther King, Jr., who electrified the country with his candidacy and rallied even the most somnolent observer with his message. "Our time has come," Jackson announced. "From freedom to equality, from charity to parity . . . from aid to trade, from welfare to our share, from slave ship to championship—our time has come." All these candidates—all preying on Mondale's weaknesses.

By the time the primaries ended and Mondale announced that he finally had enough delegates to guarantee his nomination, it was difficult to know how the "positives" could outrank the "negatives" of the Democratic battle. For a brief moment at the convention, it appeared that they might. Upbeat from the start, the convention witnessed a

 ## The First True Television President

Ronald Reagan, the Great Communicator, the Teflon President, is as well known for his effectiveness as a communicator as for the substance of what he communicated. More than any other modern political actor, Reagan understood the importance of mass-media communication. He understood how media work, how to use that to his advantage, and how to structure his appeals to communicate best through television, the dominant medium. As one analyst notes, "Ronald Reagan is our first true television president. His persona, messages, and behavior fit the medium's requirements in terms of form, content, and industry demands. Reagan made television the instrument of governing. His presidency provides the blueprint for public esteem and popularity."

Reagan, and his staff, understood that much of politics is theater, and they designed a presidency capable of taking full advantage of that understanding. This involved both relations with the media and appeals designed for the public. In dealing with the media, Reagan and his people understood that the national parade of eloquent orators. Mario Cuomo, the Italian-American governor of New York, started it off by celebrating the pride of immigrants who had risen from poverty to middle-class respectability. Jesse Jackson preached to the nation, pleading for love between brothers and sisters of all races. Mondale himself rose to the occasion. Knowing he had to act boldly if his party was to have a chance, he chose Geraldine Ferraro to be the first woman ever nominated by a major party for the vice-presidency. The American people seemed to like what they saw. For the first time in more than a year, polls ranked Mondale even with Reagan.

The Teflon President

Yet in retrospect, the very idea that anyone could have defeated Ronald Reagan seems bizarre. The economy was

---

media corps, despite its reputation for aggression, is in reality "fundamentally passive." Reagan understood that if he timed events in a certain way, then he could force coverage or cripple it, depending on his own agenda. Unlike either Ford or Carter, Reagan did not play into the requirements of the media; he forced the media requirements to play into his agenda, and thus maintained control. . . .

[There] was a particularly strong dynamic when the media encountered a president as publicly popular and amiable as Ronald Reagan. In challenging him, the media ran the risk of being perceived by the public as hounding the president in an undignified manner, instead of pursuing presidential accountability. This was a problem the Reagan administration did its best to magnify. Reagan was very aware of the importance of staging, and of how to manage it to maximize his interests and minimize those of the press. The press was kept at a distance from the president, forcing them to yell questions as he passed, sometimes over the sound of a helicopter rotor. In addition, news conferences were rare and were used for calculated effect.

Mary E. Stuckey, *The President as Interpreter-in-Chief*. Chatham, NJ: Chatham House, 1991.

booming, inflation was down, America was strong again. In the summer of 1980, before Reagan was first elected, Americans had been held hostage in Iran, United States athletes had boycotted the Moscow Olympics, the economy was paralyzed, and American morale had sunk to its lowest level since the Great Depression. Now all that had changed. Americans swept the gold at the Los Angeles Olympics (helped no small amount by the nonparticipation of Soviet and Eastern European athletes), a new patriotism permeated the body politic, and America had demonstrated its strength—once and for all—in Grenada. Nothing seemed impossible any longer. "Just about every place you look," said one Reagan ad showing a man painting a white picket fence, "things are looking up. Life is better— America is back—and people have a sense of pride they never thought they'd feel again." As one Reagan advisor observed, "I almost feel sorry for Mondale having to go up against this . . . it's like running against *America*."

As if by magic, Reagan remained untouched even by his mistakes. He was a "Teflon president," Congresswoman Pat Schroeder of Colorado said. Nothing stuck to him. Americans had long since accepted Reagan's unfamiliarity with facts, one presidential advisor noted. "What's wrong with it if the system works and people are happy. Ronald Reagan is part of the mythology of what America likes its leaders to be." If Reagan had been Nixon, one Republican wag commented, he would have been dead because people blamed *everything* on "Tricky Dick." But Reagan was the "gipper." He "never lost that quality of next-door neighborliness and never became part of the system," a journalist noted. He was a "cultural democrat," still "playing best friend, a citizen cast up among politicians." Reagan had been made into "the personification of America," *The New Yorker's* Elizabeth Drew commented. In that context, "to suggest that anything is wrong with him is to run down the country." Indeed, it was precisely that chemistry that made the president invulnerable. As one of Mondale's leading advisors observed, "you couldn't touch Reagan without hurting yourself."

In the face of such odds, Mondale could only go back to the basics of the Democratic faith, hoping to plant a seed, if not reap the harvest. In Reagan's America, he told one audience in Cleveland, "it's all picket fences and puppy dogs. No one's hurting, no one's alone. No one's hungry. No one's unemployed. No one gets old. Everybody is happy." But there was another America, Mondale said, where the poor, the disabled, the unemployed, the victims of discrimination, were treated as part of the family and were helped. That America, Mondale insisted, believed in community and compassion. Such people, Mondale allowed himself to think, would not cast a vote for selfishness dressed up as patriotism.

But in the end, there was no gainsaying the president's popularity. In a devastating landslide, he rolled to re-election with 59 percent of the vote and 49 of the 50 states. In almost every single category where Reagan appeared vulnerable, he triumphed instead. Women gave him 57 percent of their vote, the elderly 61 percent, the young—for the first time in decades—voted Republican. Catholics voted for the president; more Jews voted Republican than ever before; and even union households—where Mondale hoped for his strongest support—split almost down the middle. Only blacks, who suffered more under Reagan than any other group, remained united against him. It was a night, *Newsweek* correctly said, "that Ronald Wilson Reagan became Mr. America."

Americans Were Confident About the Economy and the Nation

Whatever the momentary analyses of the pundits, the 1984 election ultimately was as much about traditional values—and America's sense of confidence in itself—as about the prosperous economic state of the union. The two were clearly connected. If America in 1984 had been where it was in 1982, with a 10 percent unemployment rate and little prospect of recovery, Reagan might well have been defeated. But instead the economy was on the move and there was a new sense of pride and confidence about the nation's stance in the world. This latter mood was difficult to quantify, but in many ways it held the key to the election. At the end of the Carter years, 75 percent of Americans said they no longer felt confident that the future would be better than the past. Now, after four years of Reagan, more than half had returned to their traditional optimism. In 1980 only one-fifth of all Americans said that the government was run for the benefit of all. Now, in 1984, that figure had more than doubled, notwithstanding the redistribution of wealth that had taken place *away* from the poor and *toward* the rich. Reagan's campaign slogan, "We Brought America Back," seemed to resonate. His ability to link the Olympic triumphs of Los Angeles with a new sense of national assertion in the world appeared to make sense. "Let's take our cue from our . . . athletes," he declared. "Let's go for growth, let's go for the gold." And Americans responded. There was, one commentator said, "a new patriotism" abroad in the land, "growing out of a natural desire to *feel better* about things after Watergate, Vietnam and the hostage crisis." Reagan embodied this new patriotism, and brought it to fulfillment in his campaign, from the speech he gave on the beaches of Normandy commemorating the sacrifices of American soldiers on D-Day, to his proud display of America's Olympic triumphs, telling the voters that their athletes were "living proof of what happens when America sets its sights high." Whatever its intrinsic shortcomings, the Reagan credo had succeeded in winning the ardent support of millions of people inspired with a new faith in themselves and in their country. The question at the beginning of the second term was whether that faith could be sustained, and whether those entrusted with its mission would be adequate to the task.

The Iran-Contra Affair

Peter B. Levy

November 1986 marked the beginning of the biggest White House scandal since Watergate. The Iran-contra affair, as it was soon dubbed, presented grave political troubles for Reagan, who prior to it had been one of the most popular presidents of modern times.

First, reports surfaced that Reagan had secretly authorized a plan to sell arms to Iran in exchange for hostages held by pro-Iranian groups in Lebanon. This violated the U.S. policy of not negotiating with terrorists as well as Reagan's own promise that he would "never deal with terrorists." It also created foreign policy problems because officially the United States supported Iraq in the Iran-Iraq war. In the second part of the scandal, millions of dollars made from the arms-for-hostages deals were secretly funneled to the contras, a group of rebels fighting against the Communist-backed Sandinista government of Nicaragua, despite the fact that Congress had expressly forbidden further aid to the contras. Top officials in the Reagan administration had broken the law, and, as York College history professor Peter B. Levy explains in this entry from his *Encyclopedia of the Reagan-Bush Years*, a lengthy series of investigations followed.

The Iran-contra affair was not just one incident, but a number of interrelated developments that came to haunt the Ronald Reagan administration during its last three years in office. The affair continued to linger on in a more muted manner throughout George Bush's tenure as president, it had two roots. First, the president authorized an attempt by the National Security Council to sell arms to Iran in exchange for the release of American hostages held in Lebanon. Second, top Reagan administration officials decided to divert some of the proceeds from these arms deals to contra rebels in Nicaragua. Both these activities were covert operations; the latter may have been illegal. The affair grew in significance when Reagan administration officials initially lied to Congress about specific details of each endeavor. To make matters worse, the president initially denied knowledge of these developments, although he later took responsibility for them. As the public learned from the press and mass media the details of the operations themselves and of possible lies to Congress, several investigations were launched, most prominently, a presidential investigation headed by former Texas Senator John Tower, joint congressional hearings, and a very long investigation headed by Special Prosecutor E. Lawrence Walsh.

Arms for Hostages

The decision to trade arms to the Iranians for hostages was made in December 1985 by President Reagan. This action contradicted the administration's public policy of not acquiescing to the demands of terrorists. The arms deals were conducted through third parties and were initially denied by the president. Governmental officials subsequently testified that one of the goals of the arms deals was to improve relations with moderates in Iran. Millions of dollars of arms were sold without solid results. The hostages were either not released as promised or their release came only after additional dealings and negotiations. To make matters worse, there was no evidence that the exchange augmented the position of moderates in Iran. Furthermore, not all the money that was exchanged during the deals could be accounted for. Some disappeared from Swiss bank accounts where the money for the arms was funneled.

Even before Reagan approved of the arms-for-hostages deal, the administration had already solicited funds for the contras from foreign nations. This allowed the administration to claim that technically it was in compliance with the Boland Amendment, which banned federal funding for the contras except for humanitarian purposes. Whether President Reagan explicitly approved of a plan to take money derived from the arms-for-hostages deal and provide it to the contras is still unclear. Without a doubt, Colonel Oliver North, [national security adviser from 1983 to 1985] Robert (Bud) McFarlane, [CIA director] William Joseph Casey, and other top officials believed that the president approved of such a plan, at least in its broad outlines if not in fine detail. For instance, during congressional hearings, Oliver North admitted that he had negotiated a deal with the Iranians whereby they would receive 1,000 Tube-launched missiles (TOW) in exchange for the release of hostages in Beirut and about $6 to $10 million. North then testified that he took these funds and gave them to Richard Secord, a retired army general, who bought weapons to trade for the hostages.

The Scandal Breaks

When rumors of such deals first surfaced, the administration had denied them. However, as more information was released, the administration's denials became less and less credible. Finally, in March 1987, President Reagan, in a public address, took full responsibility for his actions and those of his administration. However, this pronouncement only came after the Tower Commission had issued a report that chastised the administration for its lax control over the operations of the National Security Council and after Colonel Oliver North, a central figure in the affair, had been forced to resign. Indeed, various figures in the affair, from Presidents Reagan and Bush to Secretary of Defense Caspar Willard Weinberger and Colonel North, continued to present conflicting interpretations and testimony regarding the specific responsibility and culpability of individuals well into the 1990s. During nationally televised hearings before Congress, North gained fame by claiming that he simply was following the orders of the president, while at the same time arguing that the actions were justifiable. At the time, President Reagan denied that he knew of many of the specifics of the affair, including the decision to divert funds to the contras. Likewise, George Bush denied that he was privy to major policy decisions regarding the affair, although other parties involved claimed that he was. The sudden death of Central Intelligence Agency (CIA) director William Casey, who seemed to be at the center of the covert operations, complicated the situation.

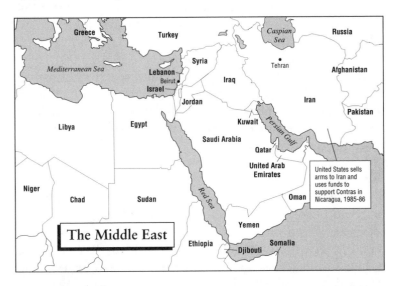

The Middle East

United States sells arms to Iran and uses funds to support Contras in Nicaragua, 1985-86

Ultimately, North, [national security adviser from 1985 to 1987] John Marlan Poindexter, McFarlane, and General Richard Secord were indicted, tried, and convicted on charges stemming from the Iran-contra affair. Many of the convictions were subsequently overturned on technical grounds—namely, that the special prosecutor had relied on information obtained by congressional investigators while under grants of immunity to obtain the convictions. In his final report, Special Prosecutor Lawrence Walsh harshly criticized the president and many of his top aides. By the time the report was issued, however, public interest in the affair had died, Walsh himself had become a target of criticism for his overzealousness in the case, and North had become a champion of the New Right for his defiance of Congress and his patriotic zeal.

Perhaps the most difficult part of the Iran-contra affair to calculate is its political costs. To an extent, the affair damaged the Reagan administration, diminishing the president's image as a "teflon president" invulnerable to personal criticism. The affair certainly emboldened Democrats in Congress, as they overrode several of Reagan's vetoes of domestic reform bills. However, on his retirement, Reagan's approval ratings were very high, suggesting that he managed to survive the Iran-contra affair with his standing relatively untarnished. In addition, George Bush managed to deflect all attempts to turn Iran-contra into a political issue in 1988. Moreover, Oliver North managed to turn his commitment to the cause of the contras and open hostility toward congressional meddlers into a political asset. Thus, despite the fact that the affair involved numerous top Reagan administration officials, represented a possible violation of the law by the president, and achieved little in terms of foreign policy objectives, it had remarkably little long-term impact on the Reagan presidency, especially when compared to the effect that similar scandals, such as Watergate, had on previous presidents.

Brief Chronology of the Iran-Contra Affair

Dec. 1981. Executive order authorizing the CIA to covertly aid Nicaraguan contras signed by President Reagan.

Dec. 20–21, 1982. Congress passes Boland Amendment restricting funding of the contras.

Feb.–Aug. 1985. Colonel Oliver North arranges for purchase of arms for hostages by private and foreign sources. Reagan states that North and others are providing only military advice.

Nov. 19, 1985. North assumes responsibilities for plan to

sell arms to Iran in exchange for hostages held in Lebanon.

Apr. 4, 1986. In memorandum to new National Security Adviser, John Poindexter, for Reagan's eyes, North proposes funneling profits from the arms-for-hostages deals to contras.

Oct. 5–9, 1986. Eugene Hasenfus, American CIA operative providing arms to contras, shot down over Nicaragua by Sandinistas.

Nov. 3–19, 1986. Reports of arms-for-hostages deal broken by press. Reagan ends exchange.

Nov. 25, 1986. North and Poindexter dismissed by Reagan after Edwin Meese III announces that some of profits from arms-for-hostages deal were diverted to the contras.

Dec. 19, 1986. Special prosecutor, Lawrence Walsh, appointed to investigate Iran-contra affair.

Feb. 16, 1987. Tower Commission issues report. It criticizes management of National Security Council but finds no criminal wrongdoing on the president's part.

Jul. 7–15, 1987. Congressional investigations of Iran-contra affair come to a climax with nationally televised testimony and questioning of Oliver North.

Nov. 18, 1987. Congressional report claims that President Reagan is ultimately responsible for Iran-contra affair. Republicans on committee reject this stern conclusion.

Apr. 7, 1990. Poindexter convicted of perjury.

May 4, 1990. North convicted of obstructing justice.

Jul. 20, 1990. North and Poindexter's convictions overturned on technical grounds.

Dec. 24, 1992. Former Defense Secretary Caspar Willard Weinberger is pardoned by President Bush. (He was under indictment for perjury.)

Jan. 18, 1992. Special prosecutor issues final report. While the report finds that neither Reagan nor Bush committed any criminal activities, it is sharply critical of the Reagan administration for deceiving Congress and the public about the affair.

CHAPTER 2

The End of the Cold War

AMERICA'S DECADES

The Reagan Doctrine and the New Cold War

Richard V. Allen

In the late 1970s, U.S. foreign policy experts theorized that the Soviet Union could not afford an extended arms race with the United States, and that the United States should begin an expensive military buildup to expose the weakness of the Soviet economy. Although the actual buildup began under Carter, the arms race reached its height under Reagan, and its justification became known as the Reagan Doctrine.

In the early years of his presidency, Reagan was very vocal about his anti-Communist views; this, combined with the arms race and Reagan's plan for a Strategic Defense Initiative—an attempt to create a space-based defense against nuclear attack—contributed to worsening relations between the two rival superpowers. In this excerpt from a 1995 speech, Richard V. Allen, former chief foreign policy advisor to Reagan, details his view that the Reagan Doctrine ultimately helped win the Cold War.

I am going to talk about how Ronald Reagan and his team—a team widely characterized at the time, both here and abroad, as a group of inexperienced and impractical right-wing ideologues and fanatics—prevailed in the Cold War. In doing so, I shall not be so foolish as to claim

Reprinted from Richard V. Allen, "The Man Who Changed the Game Plan," *The National Interest*, no. 44, Summer 1996, with permission of *The National Interest*, Washington, D.C. Copyright © The National Interest.

for them all the credit for victory. Clearly, much belongs to earlier American statesmen, from Harry Truman on; and one cannot deny a little to Mikhail Gorbachev, however unintended the consequences of his actions. But I shall offer what I believe is a reasoned defense of the proposition that the Reagan presidency can properly claim the lion's share of the credit—and, even more shocking for some, that the key factor in the winning side's team was the president himself.

Some of Reagan's critics still cannot understand how America and the world survived the eight years of his two administrations. After all, how could an aging actor, so untutored in the finer ways of thinking, so divisive and so right-wing in outlook, so unfamiliar with life inside the Beltway, [i.e., not a Washington political insider] be expected to tiptoe through (and a preference for tiptoeing was the very mark of sophistication for such critics) the nuanced strategic and diplomatic world of the 1980s? How could he run the world with his absurd 4×6 cue cards and a TelePrompTer?

Confrontation with the Soviet Union

Now it is true, President Reagan did initially take us into a confrontation with the Soviet Union. But he did so intentionally, deliberately, and in slow motion. Moving to confront the adversary in this way, Reagan followed a plan that he had thought through over many years. There were, of course, major glitches, detours, and reversals, but he never changed his basic outlook . . . and he did understand the importance of keeping it simple.

The fact that Reagan was prepared to use confrontation in this way is what has given credence to the view that, far from ending the Cold War, he actually prolonged and deepened it. There is a considerable body of revisionist history on this subject, including the work of our present deputy secretary of state, Mr. Strobe Talbott, the architect of the present administration's policy toward Russia and its former empire. One cannot help feeling that had Mr. Talbott been around in 1946, when Winston Churchill delivered his famous "Iron Curtain" speech at Fulton, he would have enthusiastically joined the many who accused Churchill of being a "warmonger."

When Churchill made that speech, we were busily demobilizing and withdrawing from Europe while Stalin stayed there, which meant that the United States was put in the position of reacting to Soviet advances in the postwar period, rather than seizing the initiative. It was only slowly and after much provocation—when, one after another, the Eastern European countries were taken over by a combination of highly effective internal subversion and external Soviet military pressure, and the Red Army did not budge from the eastern part of Germany—that the United States decided to react in earnest. When it did so, a long-term strategic plan began to take shape. . . .

Remember that [Paul Nitze] was the principal drafter of the 1950 document known as NSC-68. Signed by President Truman forty-five years ago, this landmark paper originated the policy of containment of the USSR. *How* we moved to contain the Soviet Union in various ways was a matter for successive presidents to decide, but this doctrine of containment remained essentially in place for the next forty or so years under both Republican and Democratic administrations.

In my view, however, the stage had been set for a deviation from containment and an eventual showdown with the Soviets—the showdown that was to come with Reagan in the 1980s—as long ago as the Cuban Missile Crisis of October 1962. While we breathed a collective sigh of relief in the wake of that crisis, two trends of great importance were set in motion by it. The first was the clear realization on the part of Nikita Khrushchev that, in October 1962, the Soviet Union was decidedly inferior to the United States in terms of military power. He vowed that it would not remain so, and embarked on the largest military buildup in history. We underestimated and misread this trend—badly.

The second trend was that the Chinese moved into an

open and bitter dispute with the Soviets. I believe we badly misread the implications of this trend as well, for we concluded that the so-called responsible and sober Soviets were to be contrasted with the reckless and revolutionary Chinese, who were busy promoting "wars of national liberation" in the Third World and generally undermining U.S. interests. Of course, in reality it was the Soviets who were reckless, embarking upon a huge military buildup and themselves fomenting revolutionary strife in the less-developed world; while the Chinese talked a good game of revolution, but were in reality sober and careful not to extend themselves beyond their borders.

The Era of Détente

What was to occur later in the Nixon-Ford years is surely the subject of another discussion. Let me simply note that when détente became a policy, rather than merely a descriptive statement and a generalized hope, it amounted to little more—or less—than a reaffirmation of containment. Leading practitioners of détente (and especially Henry Kissinger) seemed to believe that the United States could never entertain a notion of "winning" the Cold War, and should instead seek the best arrangement possible under less than ideal circumstances. In fact, some believed that the Soviets were actually winning and that this necessitated a deal.

In 1976, you will recall, Ronald Reagan's primary campaign caught fire when he unleashed a powerful assault on the policy of détente, and the battle became so intense that Gerald Ford nearly lost the nomination at the Kansas City convention. So heated did things become that Henry Kissinger almost did not go to the convention, and when he did, it was to be booed by many of the delegates and to be met by a Republican platform that contained a repudiation of "détente" as the centerpiece of U.S. policy toward the USSR. (That platform document never saw the light of day; it was quietly deep-sixed by the Ford administration in its losing re-election campaign.)

Even in 1976, and for as long as I knew him, Ronald Reagan rejected the doctrine of "containment." This is not to say that he repudiated or demeaned its achievements, but that he believed deeply in its inadequacy if we were ever to be secure in the modern world. He believed in developing momentum through strength, and applying that momentum to the Cold War equation. He knew that it would entail risk, but in his view a worthwhile and manageable risk, one that stopped short of outright provocation or war in order to achieve victory. He believed that a quantum change in East-West relations was necessary: no more passivity, no more reacting to Soviet initiatives, as we were clearly doing in the Carter years in Central America, Angola, and Afghanistan. He believed, simply, that democracy and freedom, resolutely asserted and eloquently articulated, could ultimately prevail.

Attempting to Gain the Upper Hand

Thus Reagan entered office in early 1981 with a clear strategy in mind. And that strategy, developed over the several years preceding his election, was, if we may use classic Soviet terminology, to change "the correlation of forces" in the world.

Reagan's program for dealing realistically with the Soviet Union was essentially a matter of getting the U.S. economy in shape, forging ahead with a comprehensive domestic program, strengthening America's defense capabilities through a sustained program of re-armament using modern and advanced technologies, and changing dramatically the way in which the country's foreign policy was conducted. There were those who said that Reagan "didn't have a clue" about how to conduct a coherent foreign policy. But he actually had more than a clue; he had a plan, and the resolution to put it into effect.

The major shift in U.S. policy was made formal in late 1982 and early 1983, through the adoption of NSDD-75, still today a secret document. The United States would no longer be content merely to shape and influence Soviet behavior, but would set out to change the Soviet system itself, and literally "roll back" Soviet advances and conquests outside its borders. The objective was to find weak points in the Soviet structure, to aggravate the weaknesses, and to undermine the system. This represented a sea change in U.S. policy.

A defense buildup would take a long time, Reagan knew, and it would be necessary to mobilize broad support for one. This he achieved by mid-year 1981, making choices for weapons and defensive systems and upgrades that sent a strong, unmistakable signal to adversaries and allies alike. Europe, with the clear exception of Mrs. Thatcher, did not much like what it was hearing; the United States was "rocking the boat", taking needlessly risky—even reckless—positions. It was "destabilizing" and "confrontational", "threatening" and "provocative." Establishment Washington agreed, and when Reagan said that communists would "lie, cheat, and steal" to get what they wanted, it went into a spasm of fright. Even some leading members of his own administration were said to be appalled at this bluntness. For their part, the Soviets sat up and took notice, and began to worry.

The Arms Race and Disarmament

There is a widespread but inaccurate view that President Reagan was transfixed by weapons, that he sought a military buildup in the belief that these weapons would be deployed and used. That is not so. He was, in fact, fundamentally a disarmer, so much so that by the time he got to the Reykjavik meeting with Gorbachev in the fall of 1986, some thought he nearly went overboard in that direction. He fervently believed that the doctrine of Mutual Assured Destruction, with its acronym "MAD", for so long the core of our declared nuclear doctrine, was fundamentally flawed and morally bankrupt because it offered the American people as hostages in a constant upward-spiraling arms race.

He believed the proper strategy to be one of clearly gain-

Reagan's Abhorrence of Nuclear Weapons

Reagan held to a very broad strategy for dealing with the Soviets, which he had enunciated even before coming to office: build up U.S. military power and then negotiate from a position of strength. But he was not a tactician and was often uninterested in and even uncomprehending of the details of the negotiations themselves. Whatever others might think, Reagan saw no contradiction between speaking his mind against godless communists in Moscow and seeking to establish a working relationship with them, or between starting a new high-technology program that would negate the very basis of Soviet military power and at the same time seeking to persuade Moscow to make large-scale cuts in its nuclear weapons arsenal.

Reagan's denunciation of the Soviet Union as "an evil empire" was probably the most famous bit of oratory that this rhetorically inclined President ever uttered. But while it was cited in praise or condemnation hundreds of times by others, Reagan himself hurled his celebrated epithet at Moscow only once, on March 8, 1983, before the annual convention of the National Association of Evangelicals at Orlando, Florida. Reagan never repudiated the statement, but he also never repeated it. . . .

However, the catchy phrase "evil empire" seemed to sum up Reagan's early view of the Soviets in a world of black and white. Moreover, it was an allusion to the popular 1977 George Lucas film, *Star Wars,* a futuristic morality play about the struggle to wrest control of a galaxy from a threatening and immoral "empire," and its 1980 sequel, *The Empire Strikes Back.* Reagan's address to the Evangelicals was dubbed by the press the "Darth Vader speech," after the villain in the Lucas films.

Much has been written about the origin of the Strategic Defense Initiative, which quickly became known as the "Star Wars" plan, and which became a central issue in U.S.-Soviet nuclear arms negotiations. The key point in nearly all the accounts is that even before entering the White House, Reagan was uncomfortable with nuclear deterrence based on the principle of mutual assured destruction, in which each side checks the other with the threat of annihilation. He was fascinated with the prospect of a technological breakthrough that would create hardware that could stop incoming missiles. . . .

On July 31, 1979, almost eighteen months before becoming President, Reagan visited the North American Aerospace Defense Command NORAD), the underground nerve center responsible for defense against nuclear missile attack. There he discovered to his shock and dismay that there was no defense against even a single Soviet missile fired against the United States. According to Martin Anderson, who accompanied Reagan to NORAD and later served on his White House staff, Reagan left the command post shaking his head with dismay and worried that as President he would have only two choices "to press the button or do nothing"—if there was a nuclear missile attack. . . .

Reagan was informed that at least 150 million Americans would be killed in a nuclear war with the Soviet Union, a horrifying prospect. Reagan, who sponsored the most massive peacetime military buildup in U.S. history, was no secret dove. He was, however, deeply opposed to the possession and use of nuclear weapons, despite the fact that they had become the central ingredient in U.S. military power. Reagan stated his antinuclear weapons views on many occasions but, strangely enough, it was a shock when they later surfaced in negotiations with the Soviet Union. Most officials of the administration, as well as much of the public, did not take his anti-nuclear weapons statements seriously because they seemed dreamy and impractical for a U.S. president, especially one with Reagan's anticommunist policies and hard-edged oratory.

Don Oberdorfer, *From the Cold War to a New Era: The United States and the Soviet Union, 1983–1991*. Baltimore: Johns Hopkins University Press, 1998.

ing the upper hand, and there negotiating from a position of strength—and the last part of that strategy, negotiation, was as important as the first. That the idea of seeking military superiority reduced the arms control community to a state of funk was of little concern to him; he aimed to build up this country's strength by relying on its economic and technological advantages, and translating those elements into measurable national power—all in order to convince the other side that it was hopelessly expensive, even impossible, to keep abreast. Only when the other side was so convinced, he reckoned, would it agree to come to the table. In other words, he believed that to disarm safely we first had to arm ourselves, deliberately and persuasively: the same sermon, not so incidentally, that Churchill had preached at Fulton.

Accordingly, by mid-1981, the president decided to move ahead with the deployment of a dazzling array of weapons systems: the B-l bomber, Stealth technology in several forms, the goal of a 600-ship Navy, dramatic new cruise and intermediate-range missiles, the M-X missile, new Trident submarines, heavy R&D [research and development] funding, and more. In the first six years of this program, the U.S. procured 3,000 combat aircraft, 3,700 strategic missiles, and 10,000 tanks. In his 1991 book, *The Turn*, Don Oberdorfer quotes Rodomir Boigdanov of Moscow's Institute for the Study of the USA & Canada as saying, "You Americans are trying to destroy our economy, to interfere with our trade, to overwhelm and make us inferior in the strategic field." He was a perceptive man.

Reagan approached the Soviets on a dual track when it came time to decide whether to deploy intermediate range and cruise missiles in Europe in mid-1981. After several long, complex, and even heated discussions in the National Security Council (NSC), in which he met with resistance from surprising quarters inside his own administration, the president simply signed off on the option he wanted from the beginning, clearly signaling with hints and body language that he wanted a consensus position: The United

States would deploy and at the same time negotiate intensely to make that deployment unnecessary.

As he was recuperating from the bullet that nearly took his life on March 30, 1981, President Reagan reached for pen and paper to hand-write a private letter to Leonid Brezhnev. In that and subsequent letters, as well as by his actions, Reagan tried to convey to Brezhnev both his belief that continuing an arms race would be counterproductive, and, that if there had to be one, the United States intended to win it. Brezhnev never understood the level at which Reagan made his appeal, and the responses always came back as Soviet boilerplate and bluster. By then the Soviets were clearly both baffled and alarmed at what they were seeing.

The Arms Race and the Soviet Economy

Reagan knew that he would have to squeeze the Soviets slowly and gently, but so they could feel it, as the U.S. programs to re-arm and modernize the military sector gained momentum. He never believed, as did many Western observers—including alleged experts—that the Soviet economy had the capacity to extract from its citizens limitless sacrifice for the sake of maintaining invincible military power. He knew instinctively that a healthy, growing, and productive American economy, with its scientific and technological excellence, would easily outpace the bankrupt "scientific socialist" system of the Soviet Union.

One of his key concerns was to deny the Soviet Union access to advanced technology. The objective would be to shut down, to the extent possible, the flow of scientific and technological data that migrated, legally and illegally, to the Soviet side. Some of it was simply stolen by a massive Soviet effort, and that would be difficult to stem. But much of it was sold openly, and Reagan was determined to put a stop to this, and to persuade the allies to follow suit. Accordingly, Bill Casey, the director of central intelligence, and others engaged in a major effort to close the doors from the United States and to persuade or, if necessary, cajole and pressure, our friends and allies in Europe and Japan to follow suit. It wasn't well received in Europe, as governments there really wanted to continue business as usual with the East, and resented U.S. interference. It wasn't always successful either, but the efforts during the Reagan years were persistent, even dogged, and people like Fred Iklé and Richard Perle at DOD, and Roger Robinson at NSC, worked hard with Casey to impede the eastward flow.

The weakness and inflexibility of the Soviet command economy were key factors in the Reagan strategy. To the extent that U.S. initiatives would place strains on that cumbersome machine, the Reagan administration sought to increase the pressures substantially. So, the screws were tightened, one turn at a time. At the outset of the Reagan administration, the Soviets were enjoying a bonanza through oil and gas sales to the West—for hard currency. During the 1970s, high oil prices had increased Soviet energy revenues more than tenfold. Western energy dollars were an important consideration in the ability of the Soviets to stay in the race, and so major efforts were undertaken, again principally by Bill Casey, to bring about a significant increase in global oil production in order to drive prices down. The benefit to the United States would be twofold: reducing the cost of energy to itself, while simultaneously undercutting the Soviet revenue stream. Every one-dollar drop in the price of oil meant a hard currency loss of between $500 million and $1 billion for the Soviets.

Led by Casey, this effort paid off handsomely as the Saudi government cooperated by increasing oil production from two million barrels to nine million. In short order the price of a barrel of oil fell from thirty to twelve dollars, inflicting a ten billion dollar annual "hit" on the Soviet Union. The machine tools, industrial robots, electronics, and computers that the Soviets needed to fulfill their ambitious Eleventh Five-Year Plan fell well beyond reach, and eventually put pressure on Moscow to plead for a "time out" in the arms race. They simply could not sustain a defense against the genuine and effective economic warfare being waged from Washington. A rapid succession of Soviet leaders—Brezhnev to Andropov to Chernenko to Gorbachev in relatively short order—did not make it easier for the Soviet side to respond effectively. Reagan used to say that he was trying to have a summit meeting with Soviet leaders, but it was hard to do because, as he put it, "they keep dying on me."

The Strategic Defense Initiative

The squeeze also included a new emphasis on strategic defense. Consistent with his basic views that defense is inherently superior in moral terms to offense and his abhorrence of "MAD", Reagan had long believed that the United States should not remain defenseless against a missile attack. Accordingly, a preliminary and informal study of the prospects for missile defense was begun in the first year of the administration. By 1983, an embryonic plan was ready and in late March of that year the Strategic Defense Initiative was announced. It soon became known by the pejorative term "Star Wars" and was roundly ridiculed and denounced both at home and abroad, especially by the Soviets.

Actually, it scared the hell out of the Russians. They were not sure whether they should believe it or whether it was a massive hoax. They rolled out all their propaganda tools to counter it, they blustered and threatened, but to little avail. After having worked for years since the Cuban Missile Crisis to find a breakthrough like this themselves, the Soviets had been outmaneuvered by the Grade B movie actor from California. Their antiquated command economy and pitifully weak technological base, at least fifteen years behind in computer technology, could not hope to sustain an effort against a determined and wealthy Western adversary. The necessary billions of rubles were just not there.

Afghanistan

But that was not all. The "squeeze" was also extended to other crucial fronts. The Soviets had an enormous presence and stake in Afghanistan, and the Reagan administration made the decision to engage by providing a reliable supply of money and arms to the Afghan *mujaheddin*. From late 1981 onward, the administration increased its efforts to open the flow of weapons, principally through Pakistan, and to get the Saudis and other friendly Arab states to finance that flow. Training, communications gear, intelligence from overhead satellite reconnaissance, rifles, mines, mortars, and eventually Stinger missiles for use against Soviet HIND helicopters—all of this converted the *mujaheddin* from a ragtag guerrilla outfit to a formidable military force. Heavy casualties—as many as twenty thousand by the spring of 1983—were inflicted on Soviet and Afghan regime troops, and the venture was turned into a Vietnam-like quagmire for the Soviets. The goals of U.S. policy were to inflict maximum casualties, to raise the price of the war—and to demoralize the Soviet high command. Remarkably, the war was also carried directly into Soviet Central Asia, and *mujaheddin*-supported strikes there became a veritable nightmare for Moscow. Late in 1986, after sustaining huge casualties and the loss of support from the Soviet people, Moscow retreated in defeat. . . .

So, it came to pass that the old fellow from California eventually prepared to leave Washington, his term expired. He had come to town with a game plan, simple but understandable. To be sure, it became a complex plan as elements were added to it and improvisations were made. Implementing the plan required a lot of money and a lot of courage, and in some respects it failed—as in the "loony tunes" of the Iran-Contra scandal, a tawdry sideshow to the main attraction of the struggle with the Soviets. But in the end the United States called the Soviet hand, and the Soviets and their satraps folded.

Mikhail Gorbachev: The Unexpected Reformer

Gale Stokes

In the following excerpt from her book *The Walls Came Tumbling Down: The Collapse of Communism in Eastern Europe*, Gale Stokes, a professor of history at Rice University, explains that in 1985, when Gorbachev came to power, the Soviet economy had become stagnant after years of control by corrupt, inefficient, and aging members of the Communist Party. As a result, the country faced a slew of domestic problems, and in trying to solve them, Gorbachev challenged many of the basic premises of Soviet society. His reforms had very unexpected consequences. Perestroika—Gorbachev's plan for restructuring the economy—ultimately exposed the faults of the Soviet system, and glasnost—the belief that the people should have more of a voice in government—added momentum to the efforts of Eastern bloc nations to break away from Soviet rule. Eventually in 1989 the nations of Eastern Europe did win their independence. In a 1991 coup, Gorbachev was removed from power and in December of that year the Soviet Union formally dissolved.

I n March 1985, a new leader appeared in the Soviet Union who did change direction, a substantial and unexpected change that had fateful consequences. After the in-

Excerpted from *The Walls Came Tumbling Down: The Collapse of Communism in Eastern Europe*, by Gale Stokes. Copyright ©1993 by Oxford University Press, Inc. Reprinted with permission from Oxford University Press, Inc.

competent and doddering Konstantin Chernenko, Mikhail Gorbachev was a surprising, almost unbelievable new leader. His "intellectual capacity and flexibility, his ability to learn on the job, his powers of argumentation, charismatic appeal, serenity in the midst of social turmoil, faith that turbulence will 'smooth out' in the long run, his sustained, single-minded motivation and irrepressible optimism, his energy, determination, and tactical political skill" marked Gorbachev as one of the world's most remarkable leaders in the second half of the twentieth century.[1] Even before coming to power Gorbachev had spoken of the need for "deep transformations" in the Soviet economy and of the need for "wide, prompt, and frank information" in a Socialist democracy. Almost as soon as he came to power he began speaking about the need for substantial economic reform and about the necessity for honesty in public affairs, not only in the sense of combating alcoholism or the corruption of the Brezhnev years but in the sense of bringing society into the public debate.[2] He initiated a daring foreign policy based on what he called "new thinking," proposing an entirely new European alignment in which the Soviet Union would be a partner, not an antagonist. At the close of a meeting with French president François Mitterand only seven months after taking power, Gorbachev put his goal succinctly: "The Soviet Union seriously intends to change the situation in the world."[3]

After eighteen years of the gray rule of Leonid Brezhnev and more than two years of rule by dying men, the Western world was perplexed, if not astonished. Where had this man come from? Could they believe him? Was it possible for a hyperrationalist system to restructure itself, especially one in which many ancient traditions of Russian autocracy seemed reproduced in modern guise? The initial reaction was skepticism and doubt. The United States ambassador to the Soviet Union thought that Gorbachev's words seemed new but that the substance would amount to nothing. Right-wing observers scoffed at the lack of specifics in his talk of economic reform, and more balanced analysts wondered if a system so completely demarketized could change in a way that would be acceptable to the huge bureaucracy of the ruling party. Even Gorbachev himself, when asked in February 1986 if the Soviet Union was beginning a "new revolution," replied, "Of course not. I think it would be wrong to formulate the question in those terms."[4]

The Need for Reform

The question itself suggests the wonderment of observers at this unexpected blazing star. But Gorbachev's emergence from the grayness of the Soviet bureaucracy was not, as Soviet analysts used to say, an accident. He represented a vigorous element in the Communist party that for some years had been anxious to rectify the serious economic and strategic problems they knew faced the Soviet Union at the end of the 1970s. These realists did not reject socialism, and none of them intended to destroy the Soviet Union. They began from the premise that the Soviet Union had made important progress since Stalin. When the great dictator died the Soviet economy was in a shambles, the standard of living below that even of tsarist times. The thaw introduced by Khrushchev and the efforts to improve economic performance in the late 1950s and the 1960s raised both morale and living standards in a way that Soviet citizens could readily observe. Under Brezhnev it was the peasants' turn to enter the mainstream of Soviet life, as their incomes increased and they obtained coverage under the national health plan. Increased military spending gave the Soviets an impressive space program and vastly increased their strategic power, especially under Brezhnev, who concentrated on building up the Soviet missile force and in creating a blue water navy.

The realists could be proud of other Soviet successes as well, such as the integration into city life of a phenomenal influx of new residents from the countryside and the education of its population. Before World War II some 56 million Soviet citizens lived in cities, and the overwhelming majority of workers and peasants had only four years of schooling or less. By the mid-1980s the number of Soviets living in cities had risen to 180 million, and more than 80 percent of manual laborers had finished more than four years of education.[5]

This vast social revolution had fundamental implications for the possibilities of economic and political change in the Soviet Union. Workers born around 1910 had entered the work force as manual laborers, often in agriculture, and remained primarily engaged in physical labor most of their lives.[6] Workers born around 1930 entered a somewhat more complex economy and often were employed in industry, where more than manual skills were needed. But two thirds of the workers born around 1950 entered what Soviet sociologists called the "intellectual labor force" and never encountered physical work. In other words, as the Soviet economy modernized, the kinds of problems ordinary citizens faced changed dramatically, and the skills they possessed to cope with change became more developed.

A New Generation of Leadership

A similar kind of generational differentiation existed among the leadership. In the late 1970s Jerry Hough enumerated four post-Khrushchevian leadership generations in the Soviet Union.[7] The first was Brezhnev's generation, born before 1910, the members of which moved up during the Stalinist purges. The second comprised those born between 1910 and 1918, including Yuri Andropov and Konstantin Chernenko, who were thrust upward during the war. The third generation, born between 1919 and 1926, was missing due to the horrible slaughter of World War II, thus leaving a significant educational and experiential gap between men like Chernenko and the members of the fourth generation, who were born after 1926, a group that included Mikhail Gorbachev. As early as 1959 Edward Crankshaw recognized that the men of this generation were different.[8] Party functionaries in the first two generations "survived either because they were too stupid to be considered dangerous, or because they brought sycophancy to a fine art, or because they were as cunning as the fox." The post-1926 generation, however, was "relaxed and easy in manner, often with a pleasantly ironical approach to life, and very much in touch with realities of every kind."[9]

The advance scouts of this generation, and Gorbachev was among the first of them, began to enter the top leadership in the late 1970s. By coincidence, just at this time Soviet economic growth rates began to decline for the first time since Stalin's death. The very success of absorbing the huge influx of men and women into the cities made further gains by the addition of labor problematic. Faltering in its developmental plans and needing to improve its efficiency, the Soviet Union was confronted with dynamic technological challenges that its lumbering economic system was ill-prepared to meet.

An Economy on the Verge of Crisis

The Soviet economy suffered all the usual disabilities of a command economy. Gorbachev himself outlined some of these in his book *Perestroika*, published in 1987. In the 1970s, he said, "the country began to lose momentum" because of declining efficiency, excessive use of energy and raw materials, waste of capital, poor consumer products, a wage-leveling mentality, lack of long-range planning, inability to attack important social needs such as housing, unproductive agriculture, and a decline of ideological and moral values that grew from reliance on the propaganda of success rather than on honest accomplishments and gains. Sounding more like a Western sovietologist than the general secretary of the Communist party, Gorbachev concluded that the "country was verging on crisis."[10]. . .

In 1981 Ronald Reagan began a substantial American military buildup, including later the Strategic Defense Initiative, a proposal to construct a high-tech missile defense system. Apparently about to be outspent and outengineered in the one area the Soviet Union could claim to be pre-eminent—military power—the Soviets had to face up at the same time to their wretched performance in providing consumers with usable shoes and dresses, as well as their dismal record in providing housing. In all areas, from energy production through military balance to consumer goods, it was clear to many Soviets that their economy was in trouble.

Perestroika and Glasnost

Gorbachev's selection in 1985 as general secretary instead of the Brezhnevian candidate, Viktor Grishin—it was not a foregone conclusion that Gorbachev would win—constituted an explicit decision for economic reform.[11] After a fairly slow start, Gorbachev installed changes of such magnitude that they produced the collapse of the Soviet Union he was trying to save. But Gorbachev's remark to the French journalist that he was not involved in revolution was correct, at least in terms of his aspirations. Perestroika, the Russian term for "restructuring," was not a marketizing reform, despite occasional rhetorical flourishes to the contrary. Of the four basic principles of perestroika that took shape in 1987, the first was that the Soviet economy would remain centrally planned.[12] The remaining proposals evoke eerie echoes of the 1960s: the success or failure of enterprises was to be based on economic criteria; incomes were to reflect productivity; enterprises were to be autonomous in their economic decisions; and workers were to participate in management decisions. Despite their amazement at the energy with which this fascinating new Soviet leader began putting these shopworn ideas into effect, most Western observers predicted from the beginning that perestroika would fail in substantially transforming the Soviet economy. They were both right and wrong. Perestroika did fail in reforming the centrally planned economy, but by completely disrupting the Soviet system perestroika cleared the ground for the creation of a new economy based on market principles. This unexpected result may become one of the classic examples of an unintended consequence.

Despite the sound and the fury, for the first three or four

years Gorbachev's economic reforms bore a strong familial resemblance to those of his predecessors, all of whom had come to grief over the same difficulty—genuine economic reform always threatened the position of the party and therefore always lost out. Gorbachev's originality was not that he understood this linkage—by now everyone understood it—but that he accepted the challenge that everyone else had avoided: reforming both society and the party in order to make the economic reforms work. The first tactic in the overall reform strategy was the policy of openness, or glasnost.[13] Gorbachev believed as a matter of principle that the people should have more say in how society should run, both because they were capable of adding to Soviet society and because it was the right thing to do. Glasnost "enhances the resourcefulness of the working people," he said in 1984, and "is evidence of confidence in the people and respect for their intelligence and feelings, and for their ability to understand events for themselves." Looking back on his reforms later, he said, "This is why we started everything in the first place—so a human being can feel normal, can feel good, in a socialist state. So that he will feel above all like a human being."[14] A more instrumental view might be that he hoped to draw the intelligentsia to his side by permitting them the kinds of freedoms they could only have dreamed of under previous regimes.

Stunning and Unexpected Changes

Since glasnost was contrary to decades of Soviet experience, it got off to a slow start. But the nuclear accident in Chernobyl in April 1986 shocked and mobilized the Soviet leadership, which realized that their efforts to conceal the enormity of the accident greatly increased the suffering and correspondingly decreased their credibility. The main signal that openness actually would be tolerated was the release late in 1986 of the great moral critic Andrei Sakharov from exile. By late 1986 and early 1987 previously unheard-of things started happening: new editors at a resuscitated *Novy Mir* (New World) and at *Moscow News*

began expanding the limits of censorship; daring economists suggested that real markets were needed; films critical of dictators and specifically of Stalin were taken off the
shelf and shown to enthusiastic audiences; television news
programs turned to factual reporting; even tourist maps
were redrawn correctly instead of with purposeful errors.
To a Soviet population used to massive disinformation
these simple steps were stunning. For seventy years the Soviet regime had encouraged apathy and conformity as two
of its best supports; now Gorbachev sought to shake off the
dullness, to create the excitement and enthusiasm that
would draw in the creative powers of the intelligentsia and
marshal the working enthusiasms of the people.

But still the economic reforms were stuck, blocked by the
inertia of the enormous economic and political bureaucracy.
By 1988 Gorbachev concluded that only a reform of the political system could bypass this bureaucracy and create popular enthusiasm. In a remarkable series of maneuvers he ca-
joled and browbeat the party and then the government into
creating a new Congress of People's Deputies elected on the
basis of secret ballot in openly contested elections.[15] By including "the broad masses of the working people in the
management of all state and public affairs," Gorbachev believed he would "complete the creation of a socialist state
based on the rule of law," reform the party, and legitimize
perestroika all at the same time.[16] After wooing the intellec-
tuals with glasnost, the elections would woo the people with
demokratsiya. The gratitude and enthusiasms unleashed by
these changes would create the public space in which the
needed economic reforms could be accomplished.

During 1988 and 1989 Gorbachev translated this
scheme into something resembling actuality. On May 25,
1989, a competitively elected Congress of People's Deputies
convened and in full view of an engrossed nationwide television audience proceeded to engage in bona fide political
contestation. Within two years the political chaos this contestation unleashed had so devastated the Soviet Union that
it completely disintegrated.

1. George W. Breslauer, "Evaluating Gorbachev as Leader," in *Milestones in Glasnost and Perestroyka: Politics and People,* ed. Ed A. Hewett and Victor H. Winston (Washington, D.C.: The Brookings Institution, 1991), 402.

2. Robert Kaiser, *Why Gorbachev Happened: His Triumphs and His Failures* (New York: Simon & Schuster, 1991), 78. Kaiser stresses the importance of a programmatic speech of December 1984, when Gorbachev first broached the basics of his program.

3. Pravda, October 5, 1985, as published in the *Current Digest of the Soviet Press* 37 (November 6, 1985).

4. Kaiser, *Why Gorbachev Happened,* 132.

5. Moshe Lewin, *The Gorbachev Phenomenon: A Historical Interpretation* (Berkeley: University of California Press, 1988), 31 and 47.

6. The generational differences outlined here are the work of Soviet anthropologists L.A. Gordon and V.V. Komarovskii, as discussed in Lewin, *The Gorbachev Phenomenon,* 53–55.

7. Jerry F. Hough, "The Generation Gap and the Brezhnev Succession," *Problems of Communism* 28 (July–August 1979): 1–16. Hough published pictures of only four Soviet politicians in this article on the Brezhnev succession: one showing Andropov, Chernenko, and Grishin as representatives of what he called the second generation, and one showing Gorbachev as a representative of the fourth generation. All became general secretary, except Grishin, whom Gorbachev defeated when he became general secretary. Less prescient, although acute in his analysis of generational change, was Seweryn Bialer, *Stalin's Successors: Leadership, Stability, and Change in the Soviet Union* (Cambridge: Cambridge University Press, 1980), who barely mentioned Gorbachev.

8. "Men" is the proper term here. Women had little or no impact at the higher levels of Soviet government.

9. Edward Crankshaw, *Khrushchev's Russia* (Baltimore: Penguin Books, 1959), 90–91 and 130, as quoted by Jerry Hough, *Russia and the West: Gorbachev and the Politics of Reform* (New York: Simon & Schuster, 1988), 20 and 31.

10. Mikhail Gorbachev, *Perestroika: New Thinking for Our Country and the World* (New York: Harper & Row, 1987), 18–24.

11. On the machinations that lay behind Gorbachev's selection, see Hedrick Smith, *The New Russians* (New York: Random House, 1990), 77; and Kaiser, *Why Gorbachev Happened,* 80–85.

12. Ed A. Hewett, *Reforming the Soviet Economy: Equality Versus Efficiency* (Washington, D.C.: The Brookings Institution, 1988), 349–50.

13. In Russian the word *glasnost* "is ambiguous. It conveys the idea of publicity rather than of frankness. The publication of selective reports about the weekly Politburo meeting is an example of *glasnost,* but the very fact that the reports are selective and brief shows the limits of the meaning" (Zhores A. Medvedev, *Gorbachev* [New York: W.W. Norton, 1986], 159).

14. Kaiser, *Why Gorbachev Happened,* 159 and 276.

15. The congress would then elect the actual legislative body, the Supreme Soviet.

16. Kaiser, *Why Gorbachev Happened,* 225.

Reagan and Gorbachev: From Anonymity to "Closeness"

Wesley M. Bagby

Wesley M. Bagby, a professor of history at West Virginia University, explains in the following essay that although Reagan's first term in office was marked by increased hostility between the Soviet Union and the United States, during his second term he showed an almost complete reversal of U.S. policies and attitudes toward his longtime rival. In a series of historic meetings between Reagan and Soviet leader Mikhail Gorbachev, the two nations hammered out the Intermediate-range Nuclear Forces (INF) Treaty, the first agreement in which the two superpowers promised to destroy their nuclear missiles. The relationship that these two leaders forged was a significant turning point in U.S.-Soviet relations and one of the first signals that the Cold War was drawing to a close.

Although Reagan had waged Cold War against Russia more intensely than anyone since [Eisenhower's secretary of state John Foster] Dulles, the last final years of his administration saw a remarkable thawing of relations. This relaxation of tensions occurred amid changes in Russia, in the international power distribution, and in Reagan.

In the years after World War II, the Soviet economy had grown faster than America's, raising Soviet GNP from about

20 percent to more than 50 percent of America's. But problems, including the allocation of 15 percent of its GNP (twice America's share) to the military; a bloated bureaucracy; aid to Marxist governments in Cuba, Vietnam, Angola, Ethiopia, and Afghanistan; a low birth rate; excessive alcoholism, smoking, and absenteeism; poor industrial quality control; and lagging technology slowed Soviet growth to an average of only 2 percent between 1976 and 1985, well below that of America. Reagan wrote that "in arming themselves to the teeth," they aggravated their "desperate economic problems." These difficulties reduced the appeal of Communist ideology, both within Russia and abroad.

Furthermore, the overshadowing dominance that the United States and the Soviet Union had once had over world affairs by virtue of their major shares of world production was ebbing as several other nations achieved more rapid economic growth than either superpower. As allies of each superpower asserted their independence, both camps fragmented. In the changed international power distribution, conflicts erupted, such as those between Israel and Syria, and Iran and Iraq, that were unrelated to the Cold War. America found itself embroiled with nations, such as Iran, that were also enemies of Russia, while becoming a near-ally of the world's largest Communist dictatorship, the People's Republic of China.

By 1984, Reagan's statements on the Soviet Union had grown less hostile. "The fact that neither of us likes the other's system is no reason to refuse to talk," he said. And, he added, America's military buildup had put America in such a position of strength that it was ready for constructive negotiations.

Changes in Russia's Government

Meanwhile, Leonid Brezhnev, who had presided over the Soviet Union for nearly twenty years, died. He was followed in late 1982 by Yuri Andropov, who launched a new peace offensive and arms limitation effort, but who himself died after only fifteen months in office. In February 1984, he was succeeded by Konstantin Chernenko who lived only until March 1985. His death brought to power Mikhail S. Gorbachev, fifty-four, an ardent reformer.

Determined to shake Russia out of its economic stagnation, Gorbachev declared war on alcoholism, absenteeism, and corruption. Young people, he told a Soviet audience, should get off alcohol and back to church. Calling for the introduction of elements of democracy and free enterprise, he advocated "glasnost" (openness), by which he meant freedom of information and debate in government decision making, and "perestroika," or reconstruction of Russia's economic and political system. He sought to reduce the size of the bureaucracy and to relax its controls in order to give individual enterprises more freedom to compete for profits. He also proposed that the state rent out farmland for private farming and encourage individuals to operate small businesses and to practice crafts for profit. He encouraged foreign corporations to establish enterprises in the Soviet Union.

Apparently, Gorbachev believed that the principal obstacle to fundamental economic reform was the selfish desire of the vast entrenched bureaucracy, including that of the Communist party, to hold onto power. In order to break its monopoly, he moved to introduce more democracy. In a 1988 speech, he proposed that Communists introduce "democracy and self-government into all spheres of life," emphasize freedom of speech and religion, respect "spiritual-mindedness," and strictly guarantee the rights of citizens. Many students of Russia found the degree and speed of his proposals breathtaking.

Desire to revive Russia's stagnant economy increased Gorbachev's desire to reduce international tensions and arms spending. The arms race had proved to be ruinously costly. "We need a lasting peace," he told British Prime Minister Margaret Thatcher, "to concentrate on developing our society and improving the life of the Soviet people." Renouncing the quest for military superiority, he advocated respect for the security needs of both superpowers. "It is vital," he told a Communist party meeting, "that all should feel equally secure." He proposed total abolition of nuclear weapons. Also, he sought to reduce the economic drain of subsidizing foreign revolutionary movements. While not renouncing support for wars of national liberation, he said that Russia would not initiate them: "It is inadmissible and futile," he told the Twenty Seventh Communist Party Congress, "to encourage revolutions from abroad."

However, he expressed doubt that Reagan would respond favorably to his peace initiatives. "Your president couldn't make peace if he wanted to," he said. "He's a prisoner of the military-industrial complex."

Changes in Reagan's Attitude Toward the Soviets

In April 1985, Gorbachev announced that Russia would halt nuclear testing and deployment of intermediate-range missiles. He allowed Soviet-bloc countries to develop close economic relations with the European Economic Community (EEC). In July, he removed the dour Andrei Gromyko as foreign minister and replaced him with the genial and flexible Eduard Shevardnadze.

Gorbachev's reforms made the idea of improving relations more acceptable to Reagan. In October 1985, calling for a "fresh start" in U.S.-Soviet relations, Reagan told his cabinet to suspend the use of terms such as "evil empire."

For nearly five years, longer than any president since Truman, Reagan had avoided a summit conference, but in November 1985, he met Gorbachev in Geneva. He hoped, he told the American people, to "begin a dialogue for peace." The exchange of views between the world's top communist and the world's top anti-communist was frank, and sometimes heated. To Gorbachev, Reagan was stubborn and contradictory, "not simply a conservative, but a political dinosaur." When Reagan criticized Soviet violations of human rights, Gorbachev spoke of hunger, unemployment, poor health care, and race discrimination in America. Each blamed the other for the arms race. Gorbachev charged that America's military-industrial complex fattened its profits by inducing anti-Soviet paranoia and that some Americans planned to escalate the arms race to "break down the Soviet economy." Their most heated exchanges came over the issue of weapons in space. Refusing to believe Reagan's promise to share SDI ("Star Wars") technology, Gorbachev charged that it would launch a new arms race. When Reagan told him that stationing large numbers of Soviet advisers in Nicaragua was "intolerable," Gorbachev replied that Russia was "helping people achieve freedom," while America was trying to "export counterrevolution."

Nevertheless, the meeting had some positive results. As the "human factor" came into play, they showed some desire to better understand each other. Forced to listen to hours of defense of the Communist position on the issues, Reagan realized that "potentially fatal" "myths and misconceptions" existed on "both sides of the iron curtain." Appearing to enjoy each other's company, each concluded that he could do business with the other. They agreed that "nuclear war cannot be won and must never be fought," that neither would "seek military superiority," that they would seek a reduction

President Ronald Reagan and Soviet leader Mikhail Gorbachev share a light moment during their historic 1985 meeting in Geneva, Switzerland.

of strategic nuclear weapons, negotiate on troop reduction, and renew cultural exchanges. Gorbachev considered the meeting a breakthrough. When they were photographed shaking hands, Reagan quipped: "I bet the hard-liners in both our countries are bleeding." Reagan, calling it a "fresh start," gave an enthusiastic report on the meeting to Congress, and his ratings in the polls hit a high of 84 percent.

Setback at Reykjavik

In a January 1986 speech, Gorbachev, accepting Reagan's "zero option" for intermediate-range missiles in Europe, proposed a nuclear test ban and the abolition of all nuclear weapons by the year 2000, and he offered to allow Western inspection of sites in the Soviet Union. He also proposed drastic cuts in conventional armaments. In February, he told the Communist Party Congress that the need was for "constructive, creative interaction among states and peoples on the scale of the entire world," and he called for "creation of a comprehensive system of international security."

On October 10, 1986, at Gorbachev's request that they accelerate progress on arms control, the two met at Reykjavik, Iceland. They continued frank exchanges on human rights and regional conflicts. Gorbachev proposed that they cut by half the number of strategic (long-range) nuclear weapons in each of the three main groups: submarine-launched missiles and long-range bombers, of which America had more, and intercontinental missiles, in which Russia was superior. Also, they agreed to total elimination within ten years of all Soviet and U.S. intermediate-range missiles in Europe (the "zero option"). Reagan proposed that they eliminate all ballistic missiles, and Gorbachev proposed eliminating all nuclear weapons, to which Reagan replied "that suits me fine." For a moment the world seemed close to agreement on nuclear disarmament, a prospect that Shultz called "breathtaking." But then, when an elated Reagan thought they had agreed on everything, Gorbachev insisted that all depended "on your giving up SDI." Enraged, Reagan "blew my top" and "walked out on Gorbachev."

The tentative agreement to eliminate long-range missiles died in the debacle. SDI was proving to be expensive.

Gorbachev Visits the United States

In December 1987, after Gorbachev agreed to negotiate on reducing intermediate missiles regardless of whether America abandoned SDI, he visited Washington for a summit conference. Calling for a world "which is democratic and free, with equality for all and with every nation enjoying the right to its own social choice without outside interference," he made a favorable public impression. He stopped his car to shake hands with a Washington crowd and, at a White House banquet attended by David Rockefeller, Henry Kissinger, Joe DiMaggio, Billy Graham, and Mary Lou Retton, sang along with Van Cliburn's rendition of "Moscow Nights." In a public opinion poll, 59 percent gave him a favorable rating, only 4 percent below Reagan. Someone suggested that he run for U.S. president, but he replied that he had a job. He was the first Soviet leader, said Reagan, who did not espouse "the Marxian theory of one-world Communist state." Establishing a personal relationship Reagan called "very close to friendship," he and Reagan called each other "Ron" and "Mikhail."

At this Washington summit, the two leaders signed the Intermediate-Range Nuclear Forces Treaty. They agreed to the "zero option," to remove all intermediate-range (300 to 3,400 miles) nuclear missiles from Europe, and Gorbachev agreed to destroy Soviet SS-20 missiles in Asia as well. This INF treaty required Russia to destroy 1,846 and America to destroy 846 missiles. Reagan, who, said Gorbachev had discovered a Russian saying that he quoted at every meeting—"trust but verify"—secured provisions that allowed each side to inspect the other's launching sites. Reagan insisted that the treaty be signed at precisely 1:45 on December 8, which, unknown at the time, had been chosen as a propitious time by Nancy Reagan's astrologer. The Senate approved the accord by a vote of 93 to 5. The last of these missiles was destroyed in May 1991.

Nothing is more difficult to negotiate than an arms reduction agreement. The earlier SALT treaties had set upper limits on future missile construction, but INF was the first ratified pact that required both sides actually to reduce the number of missiles. It affected only about 5 percent of the superpowers' nuclear arsenals, but it was a historic breakthrough that set a precedent for possible greater future reductions. In his diary, Reagan wrote this was "the best summit we've ever had."

Reagan Visits Moscow

Returning Gorbachev's visit, Reagan went to Moscow in May 1988 for his fourth summit in two and a half years, more than had been held by any previous president. Concrete accomplishments were slight (expanded student exchanges, fishing rights, space cooperation), but as theater the conference was spectacular. In his welcoming statement, Gorbachev said that long-held dislikes and stereotypes had abated. The seventy-seven-year-old president may have nodded off at a speech, and some of his anecdotes seemed unrelated to the issue, but he delivered his prepared speeches with surprising elan. He met with dissidents and the Patriarch, and took full advantage of his opportunities to lecture the Russians on human rights and the virtues of free enterprise and democracy. Making it clear that he favored Gorbachev's reforms, Reagan told students at Moscow University that they lived in an "exciting, hopeful time" when "the first breath of freedom stirs the air." Reagan seemed surprised that the ordinary citizens with whom he talked were "indistinguishable from people I had seen all my life on countless streets in America." He no longer believed, he said, that the Soviet Union was "an evil empire." He and Gorbachev shook hands with a crowd on Red Square (accompanied by a U.S. secret serviceman carrying the small black bag, known as the "football," that could send the signal to launch an atomic attack on Russia). In his parting remarks, he told Gorbachev that "we think of you as friends." Gorbachev said that "we've come a long way" but that "more could have been achieved." In England, Reagan said that "all of this is a cause for shaking the head in wonder. Imagine the president of the United States and the general secretary of the Soviet Union walking together in Red Square talking about a growing personal friendship . . . realizing how much our people have in common."

The Senate had rushed approval of the IMF treaty so that the leaders could sign the final version, but other concrete accomplishments at the Moscow summit were slight. The two leaders agreed to give each other twenty-four-hour notice of future missile tests and to exchange a thousand students annually. Reagan resisted Gorbachev's attempts to include in the final communique the phrase "peaceful coexistence," which right-wing Republicans had long excoriated.

"The New Closeness"

In a December 7 speech to the UN, Gorbachev, saying that foreign policy should not be driven by ideology, advocated "freedom of choice" for all nations. He announced that he would unilaterally cut Soviet armed forces by 500,000 men (20 percent) and reduce Soviet forces in Eastern Europe and the European part of Russia by 10,000 tanks, and 800 aircraft, thereby assuming a strictly defensive stance. The U.S. press praised his "vision" and "boldness." In 1989 he withdrew the last Soviet troops from Afghanistan. The Soviet navy withdrew its ballistic submarine patrols from near the U.S. coast and stopped visiting the Caribbean. Gorbachev also cut aid to the Sandinistas in Nicaragua and sought removal of Cuban troops from Angola.

Nearly all of the agreements that had been reached represented Soviet acceptance of U.S. positions. "We are going to do a terrible thing to you," said Georgi Arbatov, director of the Soviet Institute For The Study of America. "We are going to deprive you of an enemy."

In his January 1989 presidential farewell address, Reagan concluded that America had "forged a satisfying new closeness with the Soviet Union," and, he added "I want the new closeness to continue."

The Revolutions of 1989 and the Collapse of the Berlin Wall

Don Oberdorfer

The final year of the 1980s was one of the most eventful, in terms of world politics. In that year, Poland, Hungary, Czechoslovakia, and Bulgaria all broke free of Soviet rule, greatly contributing to the eventual collapse of the USSR itself in 1991. Amidst these revolutions, Hungary began allowing East Germans to cross through its territory into the democratic West Germany—thus circumventing the Berlin Wall. On November 9, 1989, television crews captured one of the most historic and emotional events of the twentieth century, as jubilant Berliners began tearing down the now-obsolete wall that had symbolized the division between Eastern and Western Europe for almost three decades. In this excerpt from his book, *From the Cold War to a New Era: The United States and the Soviet Union, 1983–1991*, Don Oberdorfer, former diplomatic correspondent for the *Washington Post*, chronicles the events that marked the "beginning of the end" of the Cold War.

W hen 1989 began, Europe was divided from East to West along the lines that had been established in the aftermath of World War II and with few exceptions frozen ever since. On the eastern side of what Winston Churchill

Excerpted from *From the Cold War to a New Era: The United States and the Soviet Union, 1983–1991,* by Don Oberdorfer (Baltimore: Johns Hopkins University Press). Copyright ©1991, 1998 by Don Oberdorfer. Reprinted with permission.

in 1946 had named the Iron Curtain, the nations of Poland, Hungary, Czechoslovakia, Bulgaria and Romania were dominated by communist parties beholden to Moscow and kept in power by the threat of Soviet military intervention, as they had been for four decades. Behind fortified barriers and watch towers snaking across the countryside and an ugly concrete and steel wall through the heart of Berlin, East Germany was a powerful half a nation, ruled by orthodox communists who had contempt for Gorbachev's reforms.

The Year of Revolution

By the end of the year, the leaders of all those nations would either change their political orientation or be ousted by popular uprisings. In every case except for Romania, hardly a drop of blood would be spilled. The armored and reinforced borders between East and West Germany would be opened, to the joy of Germans from both sides dancing triumphantly on the Berlin Wall. With dizzying suddenness, the Soviet Union's European empire, its buffer zone between Soviet territory and the West, would collapse. Rarely in history has such a sweeping reorientation of political, economic and military power taken place so swiftly without military conquest or bloody revolution.

The downfall of the Soviet dominance over Eastern Europe, with no intervention or resistance from Moscow and even hints of prodding by Gorbachev in the direction of change, would demonstrate that the Soviet Union had fundamentally changed the policies it had applied with force and determination on its periphery since World War II. Beyond the massive shift in Soviet intentions, the revolutionary developments of 1989 would also signal a sharp decline in the Soviet Union's capability to use military power beyond its borders to mount an attack in Europe. Although Soviet troops would still be in Eastern Europe in large numbers at the end of 1989, their exodus would be underway. While the popular revolutions would be still incomplete in many cases and Germany not yet reunited, it would be clear by the end of the year that none of the nations of the former Soviet empire in Europe would seek or even accept Soviet domination in the future. All this would have powerful effect on the basic requirements and premises of U.S. policy toward the Soviet Union.

How the Revolution of 1989 happened—and happened so suddenly—will be the subject of historical study and analysis for decades to come. To a greater extent than is now generally acknowledged, the peoples of Eastern Europe and those who stepped forward to be their leaders are likely to be credited as the key protagonists. Nonetheless, Gorbachev and his associates in the Soviet Union, whether by calculation or miscalculation, played a crucial role in permitting it to happen so quickly and peacefully. The Bush administration played at least a significant role through the conduct of its dialogue with Moscow and with the nations involved.

"The Brezhnev Doctrine Is Dead"

For most of his official career, Mikhail Gorbachev had had little contact with the Soviet bloc in Eastern Europe. His earliest, and for a long time probably his most important, contact with the fraternal countries was his friendship in Moscow University's law school with Zdenek Mlynar, a Czech student, who later became one of the reformist leaders of the Czechoslovak communist party during the 1968 Prague Spring. Mlynar was expelled from the party and eventually fled to the West after Soviet military intervention ended this effort at constructing "socialism with a human face." Years later he described the 1968 showdown meeting in which Leonid Brezhnev bluntly told the Czech leaders they must yield to the Kremlin's wishes. Brezhnev's logic, Mlynar wrote, was simple:

> Your country lies on territory where the Soviet soldier trod in the Second World War. We bought that territory at the cost of enormous sacrifices, and we shall never leave it. The borders of that area are our borders as well. Because you do not listen to us, we feel threatened. In the name of the

dead in World War II who laid down their lives for your freedom as well, we are therefore fully justified in sending our soldiers into your country, so that we may feel secure within our common borders. It is immaterial whether anyone is actually threatening us or not: it is a matter of principle, independent of external circumstances. And that is how it will be, from the Second World War to "eternity."

After the Czech reformers were ousted by Soviet tanks, Brezhnev issued a public justification for the action, which became known as the "Brezhnev Doctrine." In essence, it stated that a threat to the political system in any socialist country was "a threat to the security of the socialist commonwealth as a whole." In other words, once a "socialist" country, forever a "socialist" country, as long as the Soviet Union had the military power to keep it in the fraternal camp.

Twenty-one years later, in October 1989, Soviet Foreign Ministry Spokesman Gennadi Gerasimov officially declared that "the Brezhnev Doctrine is dead" and in its place offered a new hands-off policy summed up in a witty reference to American popular culture. "You know the Frank Sinatra song 'My Way'? Hungary and Poland are doing it their way. We now have the Sinatra doctrine."

Gorbachev's Initial Reforms

Even though he took power in 1985 as a reformist leader for the Soviet Union, Gorbachev did not initially suggest any change in the relationship between the Soviet Union and the Eastern European states. . . . His first foreign policy statement gave highest priority to preserving and strengthening "fraternal friendship with our closest friends and allies, the countries of the great socialist community." He quickly extended the Warsaw Pact military alliance for twenty years in a meeting with Eastern European communist leaders in the Polish capital, and seemed to suggest modest internal reforms along with strengthened discipline as a way to deal with growing disaffection in Eastern Europe. . . .

The first major issue between Moscow and the bloc countries in the Gorbachev era was whether the others

NATO and the Warsaw Pact, 1989

Iceland

Sweden

Norway

Finland

Atlantic
Ocean

United
Kingdom

Denmark

Netherlands

Ireland

East
Germany

Poland

Soviet Union

Belgium

West
Germany

Czech

France

Switzerland

Austria

Hungary

Italy

Yugoslavia

Romania

Albania

Bulgaria

Portugal

Spain

Turkey

Greece

NATO
Warsaw Pact

would be required to follow the Soviet leader's path as his reforms got underway in the USSR, according to Aleksandr Tsipko, an expert on Eastern Europe on the staff of the Soviet Communist Party Central Committee from late 1986 to 1990. Tsipko said that the issue was decided by a summit meeting of the "leaders of fraternal parties of Socialist countries," including Gorbachev, all six Warsaw Pact party leaders, Fidel Castro of Cuba, Truong Chinh of Vietnam and Jambyn Batmonh of Mongolia in Moscow in November of 1986. According to Tsipko, Gorbachev made public the essence of the results in his speech in Prague in April 1987, including this central point: "No one has a right to claim special status in the socialist world. The independence of every party, its responsibility to the people in its own country, the right to decide questions of the country's development are unconditional principles to us."

This decision had something in it for both sides of the political debate. Conservatives such as the elderly Warsaw Pact leaders at the time who had been in power for decades, and Gorbachev's conservative colleague, Yegor Ligachev, took heart that each fraternal party would not be required to implement a local version of *perestroika*. In Ligachev's words from April 1987, "Every country looks for solutions independently, not as in the past. It is not true that Moscow's conductor's baton, or Moscow's hand is in everything . . . every nation has a right to its own way." For progressives, the decision had another clearly implied and, in the end, more important meaning: that the Soviet Union should keep hands off the internal processes among its allies, whatever direction they might take, and would not bail them out if they failed to adjust rapidly enough to new realities. Just how far Soviet tolerance extended—whether to the bounds of socialism or even beyond—was an open question through the events of 1989. For many experienced outside observers, and insiders too, it was simply unthinkable that Gorbachev would permit the Eastern European states to break away from the Soviet embrace. . . .

The Fear Factor Begins to Disappear

As seen from Eastern Europe, several developments in Moscow raised doubts about Soviet determination to use force (as Moscow had done in East Berlin in 1953, Hungary in 1956, and Czechoslovakia in 1968) or the threat of force (as in Poland in 1981) to keep its regional allies in the communist camp. In making a deal to remove U.S. missiles from Western Europe under the INF Treaty, Moscow had agreed to remove its missiles from Eastern Europe. Moreover, the decision to withdraw Soviet troops from Afghanistan suggested that Moscow was ready to pull back rather than hold on to troublesome military commitments, even on its own border, and that the people and government of the Soviet Union were hardly prepared to mount new military interventions.

Perhaps more than any other single event, however, Gorbachev's appearance at the United Nations in December 1988 set the stage for the revolutionary events that would follow. Gorbachev's declaration renouncing the threat or use of force and his commitment to "freedom of choice" for all nations, a principle that "knows no exceptions," suggested that Moscow would not again send its tanks and troops into action in Eastern Europe. And his dramatic announcement of unilateral withdrawal of fifty thousand Soviet troops and five thousand tanks from Eastern Europe was an unmistakable message that the capacity as well as the will to protect Warsaw Pact regimes from their own people was sharply declining. The "fear factor" that had held Moscow's empire together for four decades was abruptly disappearing, leaving the leaders of unpopular regimes to face their people without Soviet tanks to back them up.

The Solidarity Movement in Poland

The first internal crisis came in Poland, the most politically advanced of the six Warsaw Pact regimes. [Polish head of state Wojciech] Jaruzelski's martial law regime had jailed Solidarity union activists and banned the popular anticommunist movement in 1981, but had not succeeded in destroying it. By January 1989 Solidarity was stronger than ever and Jaruzelski, amid growing economic crisis, was forced to deal with it. After a battle within the communist United Workers party, Jaruzelski moved toward opening "round table talks" intended to bring the opposition into a coalition firmly led by the communists, in return for restoring legal status to the communist world's first independent union. The Polish leader told U.S. Ambassador John Davis that he was in close touch with Gorbachev through frequent communications. There was no sign of objection or interference from Moscow.

In the negotiations with Solidarity, the communists surprisingly agreed to free elections for a new upper house of the Polish parliament, on condition that communists and their traditional parliamentary allies continue to control the more powerful lower house. The results of this unprecedented free choice, in June 1989, stunned everyone: Solidarity won ninety-nine of the one hundred seats in the new upper house; thirty-three of the thirty-five top party and government leaders lost their seats in the lower house, even though unopposed, when more than half the voters crossed out their names on the ballots.

At this juncture, President Bush paid a visit to Poland and Hungary July 9–13, his first presidential trip to the Soviet bloc. . . .

By the time of his July visit, Bush had worked out his basic orientation to the events of Eastern Europe. Poland and perhaps other nations had a good chance to win their freedom, he believed, but only with the acquiescence of the Soviet Union. An important U.S. role, he explained to aides, was to make it as easy as possible for Gorbachev to do what he had to do, and especially to avoid words or deeds that could inflame Soviet conservatives. There should be no gloating or triumphant declarations as Eastern European countries broke free of their old restraints, Bush decreed, and no insistence that the Eastern Europeans turn their backs on Moscow and join the West. He told Poles and Hungarians in private meetings during his visit, "We're not here to make you choose between East and West." While condemning the failure of the "Stalinist system" in his public statements, Bush quoted approvingly from Gorbachev on freedom of choice and told reporters he had informed Polish and Hungarian leaders that "we're not there to . . . poke a stick in the eye of Mr. Gorbachev; just the opposite—to encourage the very kind of reforms that he is championing, and more reforms.". . .

The Impossible Happens

In August the Polish situation came to a head when the Solidarity movement was struggling to form a coalition government with the defense and interior ministries reserved for the communists. At this point the Central Committee of the Polish communist party was split, with some leaders holding out for greater control of the new government and some ready to join. At the peak of the crisis on August 22, a celebrated forty-minute telephone conversation between Gorbachev and Polish General Secretary Mieczyslaw Rakowski appeared to turn the tide toward communist participation in the coalition government.

Gorbachev's telephone call has been often cited as the most tangible evidence available that he was actively pushing democratization in Eastern Europe, even at the risk to communist rule. It was reported in front page articles from Warsaw in *The Washington Post* and *The New York Times* quoting Polish communist spokesman Jan Bisztyga as saying shortly after the call that Gorbachev had encouraged communist participation in the Solidarity-led coalition. An account from Moscow by *The Los Angeles Times* based on Soviet sources said, "Gorbachev told Rakowski bluntly that the time had come to yield power." Bush publicly praised Gorbachev for helping persuade the Polish communists to join the coalition. A senior U.S. intelligence official, enunciating a widespread consensus on the historic nature of Gorbachev's intervention, told me later that "the Rubicon was crossed with the Gorbachev phone call to Rakowski. Its real meaning was that Soviet power would not be used to maintain communist power in Eastern Europe.". . .

Two days after the Gorbachev-Rakowski conversation, Solidarity adviser Tadeusz Mazowiecki was overwhelmingly elected Poland's prime minister with the communists agreeing to participate in the Solidarity-led government. He received a cordial telegram from the Soviet government.

The impossible had happened: the communists had given up power to a noncommunist government in a Warsaw Pact country, and the Soviet Union had let it happen. If it could happen in Poland it was no longer unthinkable in the rest of Eastern Europe. Communist governments were shaken, and noncommunists were emboldened everywhere. The drama in Warsaw was a precipitating event for the rest of Eastern Europe, proving the essential truth of the Czech dissident playwright (later Czech president) Vaclav Havel's observation in his book *The Power of the Powerless:*

> The moment someone breaks through in one place, when one person cries out, "The Emperor is naked!"—when a single person breaks the rules of the game, thus exposing it as a game—everything suddenly appears in another light and the whole crust seems then to be made of a tissue on the point of tearing and disintegrating uncontrollably.

Hungary Opens Its Border with East Germany

Just hours after Gorbachev's telephone call to the Polish communist party chief, Hungarian Foreign Minister Gyula Horn made a decision, after a sleepless night, that would initiate another historic change in the face of Europe. Earlier in the year, Hungary had dismantled its border fence with Austria, an act of only symbolic importance to Hungarian citizens, who already were free to travel to the West. It was more important to disenchanted East Germans, who began to make their way to Hungary in large numbers to flee through this back door to Austria and West Germany. Under a 1968 treaty with East Germany, Hungary was required to prevent such escapes, and Hungary had continued to stop Germans from leaving through its territory for the West. Now the number of East Germans, many of them young couples with small children, was building up, and Hungary was becoming a holding pen for East Germans on the run from their tyrannical government.

Horn had authorized his deputy minister, Laszlo Kovacs, to assess informally the reaction of the Soviet Union if Hungary should change its policy and let the East Germans go. "We didn't specify, but we hinted," said Kovacs. The Soviets did not object.

By the morning of August 23, Horn had decided to ignore the twenty-one-year-old treaty and open the gates to the West for the East Germans. "It was quite obvious to me that this would be the first step in a landslide-like series of events," he said later. After Horn officially informed the

East German government, which strenuously objected, Hungary announced its decision on September 10. Within three days, more than thirteen thousand East Germans fled to the West through Hungary, the largest East German exodus since the Berlin Wall was built in 1961. East Germany enlisted the help of the Czech government to stop its citizens from reaching Hungary, with the result that tens of thousands of East German refugees sought refuge in the West German Embassy in the Czech capital of Prague; eventually they were permitted to travel to the West. Next East Germany cut off travel even to Czechoslovakia, but this generated mass protests at home and redoubled the sharply rising pressure on the East German borders.

Now the hurricane gathered even more force.

In Hungary on October 7, the Hungarian Socialist Workers (communist) party officially abandoned Leninism and reconstituted itself as the Hungarian Socialist party, the first time a ruling communist party had abandoned its fundamental ideology. Later in the month, on the anniversary of the 1956 uprising, Hungary declared itself a "republic," in which Western-style democracy and democratic socialism would be practiced, rather than a "people's republic." Over the coming months the reformist communist-turned-socialist party would try assiduously to gain public favor through democratic means, but it was able to win only 8 percent of the vote in national elections in April 1990.

Massive Protests in East Germany

In East Germany the visit by Gorbachev on October 6 and 7 to celebrate the fortieth anniversary of the German Democratic Republic [GDR] added new force to the biggest nationwide wave of protest demonstrations in that regime's history. Gorbachev stood on a reviewing stand in East Berlin waving with an open palm to tens of thousands of East German youths; beside him the hard-pressed and ailing seventy-seven-year-old East German leader, Erich Honecker, pumped the night air with his clenched fist. In several cities Honecker's police attacked demonstrators who were chanting, "Gorby! Gorby! Gorby!" but the crowds of protesters became bigger each day. In East Berlin, a Western European diplomat observed a significant change in public behavior: "People are not afraid anymore to stand up and rally in masses, and proclaim their desires."

The turning point for East Germany came on October 9 in Leipzig, the second-largest city, when local communist party leaders refused Honecker's orders to attack the seventy thousand marchers who paraded through the streets. Honecker's security chief, Egon Krenz, embraced the Leipzig revolt and on October 18 led the battle within the Politburo that forced Honecker to resign. Krenz was named his successor.

The crowds of protesters only became bigger. In East Berlin on November 4, more than five hundred thousand people demonstrated, and another five hundred thousand turned out in other cities. Prime Minister Willi Stoph and his entire cabinet resigned; there was another big shakeup in the communist party Politburo. Nothing could stop or even slow the prodemocracy fever. According to several members of the GDR communist party Central Committee, Krenz called Gorbachev in Moscow to find out if the Soviets had any suggestions. These sources said Gorbachev replied that the border between the two Germanys had to be opened to provide an escape valve and prevent unrest that threatened to bring down communist control.

The Fall of the Berlin Wall

On the night of November 9, after a day of confusion, the crossing points in the Berlin Wall were flung open, never to close again. Jubilant East Germans thronged through the Wall's eight crossing points, to be met by West Berliners with champagne and fireworks. "The Wall is gone! The Wall is gone!" cried West Berliners, many of whom crossed over in the other direction. Near the Brandenburg Gate, scores of young East and West Berliners climbed to the top of the Wall to greet one another and celebrate. In high emotion, some in tears, people on both sides began to chip away at the ugly concrete and steel barrier with hammers and chisels.

Officially, the reaction in Moscow was muted. Tass said, "The pulling down of the Berlin Wall, which has symbolized the division of Europe for many years, is surely a positive and important fact." A *Pravda* correspondent in East Berlin called the move "a bold and wise political step" by the GDR government that "graphically confirms its will for renewal" along the lines of Gorbachev's "new thinking." Nonetheless, Tass and Soviet officials warned that Moscow would not tolerate the demise of the East German state, which was described as "our strategic ally," or East German departure from the Warsaw Pact alliance.

Inside the offices of communist party Central Committee in Moscow, according to staff member Aleksandr Tsipko, the reason for the low-key initial reaction was the mistaken belief that changes in the East German communist leadership "would lead to the setup of a truly democratic socialist state in Germany." The initial instructions to the veteran Soviet ambassador to the GDR, Vyachislav Kochemasov, were not to interfere, not to exert any pressure and in fact not to do anything, said Tsipko. He said it took about two weeks for Moscow to realize that the progressive weakening of the GDR and the opening of the Wall were likely to bring the collapse of the regime and its consolidation as part of the West.

The news that East Germany had decided to open its borders reached Washington in the early afternoon of November 9. At 3:30 P.M. Bush called reporters to the Oval Office for an on-camera reaction that was positive but so restrained in comparison to the almost delirious joy being seen on television that his questioners and viewers found it odd. With Gorbachev in mind, Bush said, "We are handling it [the East German move] in a way where we are not trying to give anybody a hard time." When a reporter commented that the President did not seem to be elated about this historic and unexpected victory for the West, Bush responded, "I am not an emotional kind of guy." Commented CBS anchorman Dan Rather about the President's performance, "He looked as relaxed as a pound of liver."

A Watershed Event

For nearly three decades, since its construction in 1961, the Berlin Wall had been the most visible and potent international symbol of communist tyranny. Its demise had a major effect on American opinion. Pollster Louis Harris found nearly unanimous (90 percent) public agreement that the event was "one of the most exciting and encouraging signs for peace in the world in years." Another survey, by NBC News/*Wall Street Journal,* reported that more than half the public (52 percent) saw the events in Germany and Eastern Europe as "the beginning of a long-term positive relationship" with the Soviet Union rather than "temporary and easily changed" (37 percent). The Public Agenda Foundation, which studies American opinion in depth, found a startling reversal in the views of a "focus group" of representative citizens who were interviewed in Edison, New Jersey, in mid-August (before the Wall was opened) and a similar group interviewed in San Francisco in mid-November (just after the breaching of the Wall). The consensus of the earlier group was that the changes in Eastern Europe were reversible, that the Soviet Union had control of events and would intervene if an "invisible line" was crossed, and that the reunification of Germany was impossible. The consensus of the second group three months later was that the changes in Europe were irreversible, the Soviets would not intervene and the reunification of Germany was likely.

The day after the Wall was breached, a worried Gorbachev dispatched a message to Bush and several Western European leaders expressing alarm about the breakneck speed at which events in Germany were taking place. Events in Germany should be handled slowly, Gorbachev insisted, and the interests of the Soviet Union should be taken into account. History had dictated that there be two Germanys, Gorbachev said in the message, implying that for the present era, at least, two Germanys should remain. Finally, the Soviet leader broached the possibility that events in Berlin could become violent or spin out of control; in view of this the Soviet Union suggested urgent consultations and insisted on being part of any forthcoming decision-making process. After consulting European allies, Bush sent back a vague reply, emphasizing the importance of German self-determination but not, at this point, accepting the Soviet demand for a role in decision making.

Bulgaria and Czechoslovakia Reject Communism

As the Wall was being opened on November 9, the Bulgarian communist party was holding a showdown Politburo meeting. Todor Zhivkov, Eastern Europe's longest-serving leader, planned to top off his thirty-five years in power by crushing the opposition of Foreign Minister Petar Mladenov, who had been in office nineteen years. But at the meeting, the tables were turned and the Politburo chose Mladenov rather than Zhivkov to lead the shaken party. Under Mladenov and several successors, the reform communists were able to hang on to power in Bulgaria for more than a year before finally being overtaken by democratic forces.

The events in Germany also ricocheted in Czechoslovakia, where on November 17 a student rally in Prague was attacked by nervous police. In response to police brutality and rumors that a student had been killed, demonstrations quickly escalated: 10,000 people on November 19; 200,000 on November 20; 250,000 on November 22; 350,000 on November 24. That night at an emergency communist party meeting, General Secretary Milos Jakes and his entire twelve-member Politburo resigned, and a new top party hierarchy was elected. Antigovernment forces denounced the move as a trick, bringing out even bigger crowds and a two-hour general strike that brought the capital and most of the rest of the country to a standstill.

Early in December, a reformist communist leadership promised to form a new cabinet, including a noncommunist majority. On December 10 long-time communist leader Gustav Husak, who had given up his party post to become president of the country two years before, resigned, and Czechs celebrated a new era. His eventual successor was Czechoslovakia's most renowned opposition leader, playwright Vaclav Havel.

With the triumph of the Velvet Revolution, as the Czech uprising was called, the leadership had been ousted in five of the six Warsaw Pact allies of the Soviet Union. Only Romania's Nicolae Ceausescu remained.

Brezhnev Doctrine: Mlynar on Brezhnev's thinking: Zdenek Mlynar, *Nightfrost in Prague* (Karz Publishers, 1980), p. 240. Brezhnev Doctrine: Charles Gati, *The Bloc That Failed* (Indiana University Press, 1990), p. 73.

Gorbachev's "Sinatra Doctrine": Gerasimov quote: "Ol' Bushy Brows vs. Ol' Blue Eyes," *Time*, 11/6/89, p. 42. Prague Club: William Luers, "Czechoslovakia: Road to Revolution," *Foreign Affairs*, Spring 1990, pp. 79–80; also interview with Aleksandr Tsipko, 11/16/90. "Little Gorbachevs": interview with a senior U.S. official, November 1990.

Origins of Bloc Self-Determination: See the remarks of Aleksandr Kapto of the Central Committee staff to the Foreign Ministry's Scientific and Practical Conference, as published in *International Affairs*, November 1988, p. 29. He refers to the November 1986 meeting and also to a memorandum drawn up by Gorbachev for the Politburo, apparently at that time. Ronald Asmus of the Rand Corporation, who has written extensively on the Soviet Union and Eastern Europe, believes there were two meetings with Eastern Europeans dealing with key aspects of their relationship and a Politburo meeting between the two at which major decisions were made. This possibly could have been the meeting of CEMA heads of government, including Soviet Prime Minister Ryzhkov, in Bucharest on 11/3/86, and the meeting of the Communist Party leaders of the CEMA countries in Moscow 11/11–12/86. Ligachev quote: Karen Dawisha, *Eastern Europe, Gorbachev and Reform* 2d edition (Cambridge University Press, 1990), p. 214. Ligachev told David Remnick after being ousted from the leadership that the Kremlin's "noninterference" stance in Eastern Europe had been decided in late 1985 and 1986; see David Remnick, "A Soviet Conservative Looks Back in Despair," *Washington Post (WP)*, 10/15/90, p. A1.

Crisis in Poland: Jaruzelski to Amb. Davis: Davis telephone interview 11/29/90; see also Gati, *The Bloc That Failed*, and the *WP* series "The Turning Points," published 1/14/90.

Bush's Eastern Europe Policies: No gloating, no insistence on turning their backs: interview with a senior U.S. official, 11/6/90. Bush on not being there to "poke a stick": David Broder, "Bush to Push E. Europe Aid," *WP*, 7/14/89, p. A1.

Gorbachev-Rakowski Call: A.D. Horne, "Gorbachev Urges Communists to Join Solidarity Government," *WP*, 8/23/89, p. A1; Francis X. Clines, "Gorbachev Calls, Then Polish Party Drops Its Demands," *NYT*, 8/23/89, A1. The *Los Angeles Times* account was written by Michael Parks for the issue of 12/17/89. Bush's comments: David Hoffman, "Bush Lauds Gorbachev Stand on Polish Government," *WP*, 8/24/89, p. A26.

Havel on Rules of the Game: William Echikson, *Lighting the Night* (William Morrow, 1990), p. 69.

Hungary's Decisions: Blaine Harden, "Refugees Force a Fateful Choice," *WP*, 1/14/90; Kovacs interview in Budapest, 1/3/90.

East Germany Developments: Krenz's call to Gorbachev: Marc Fisher, "One Year Later, World Is Learning How Berlin Wall Opened," *WP*, 11/10/90, p. A23. Moscow reaction at fall of Wall as seen by Tsipko: Tsipko interview, 11/16/90.

U.S. Public Opinion: Poll data: Daniel Yankelovich, *Coming to Public Judgment* (Syracuse University Press, 1991), pp. 146–47. "Focus group" data: Public Agenda Foundation, New York.

Gorbachev's Message to Bush: From a U.S. official source, 12/17/90, and background interviews with two other U.S. officials in December 1990.

The End of the Cold War

Michael Kort

In the following selection, Boston University professor of social science Michael Kort explains that as the 1980s ended, so did the Cold War that had dominated international relations since 1945. Kort summarizes the events of 1989, 1990, and 1991 and discusses some current historical debates regarding the end of the Cold War, such as the role that Reagan and Gorbachev each played, as well as the impact of nuclear weapons on international relations. Kort suggests that because of the enormous toll the conflict took on both nations, neither the Soviet Union nor the United States really "won" the Cold War.

The end of the Cold War, although not provoking the intense controversy surrounding its origins, has produced its own debates. There is no general agreement about precisely when the Cold War ended, although the signing of the Charter of Paris in November 1990 provides a logical marker for its termination, in the same way the Yalta Conference of February 1945 marks the beginning of the struggle. There is sharp disagreement about what role the United States military buildup under Ronald Reagan, and in particular his Strategic Defense Initiative proposal, played in bringing an end to the Cold War. Experts such as Samuel F. Wells contend that the Reagan administration hastened the end of the Cold War by confronting the Soviet Union with a new

Excerpted from *The Columbia Guide to the Cold War,* by Michael Kort (New York: Columbia University Press). Copyright ©1998 by Columbia University Press. Reprinted with permission from the Copyright Clearance Center.

arms race that its leadership knew it could not afford. Raymond L. Garthoff concurs with analysts who give the lion's share of the credit for the end of the Cold War to Soviet leader Mikhail Gorbachev.[1] In a similar vein, there is even a debate about who won the Cold War. There is no doubt that the Soviet Union, which collapsed shortly after the Cold War ended, was the most decisive loser. But what about the United States? The end of the Cold War and the subsequent collapse of the Soviet Union left the United States as the world's only political and military superpower. At the same time, the United States paid a tremendous economic and social price in waging and winning the Cold War. Therefore, a case can be made that, like the Soviet Union, America ended up a loser. The real winners in this scenario were Germany and Japan, losers in World War II, who during the Cold War, protected by the American nuclear umbrella, focused their energies and resources on building civilian industries and infrastructure and emerged from that era with healthier economies than that of their superpower protector. . . .

1989: The Year of the People

The Cold War began as a result of Soviet expansion into Eastern Europe and the imposition of Communist regimes on the countries of the region; its termination required that the Soviet satellites receive the right to self-determination. By 1989 the process of reform in the Soviet Union had gone farther than anyone had expected. In addition to perestroika, the changes included the elimination of totalitarian controls on information and communication, or *glasnost,* and the democratization of Soviet political life, or *democratizatsia.* What Gorbachev found out was that he could not, as he apparently first intended, administer small, controlled doses of freedom to Soviet society from his Kremlin office. To his surprise the Soviet people reacted to each dose by incessantly demanding more and within a few years the process of reform took on a life of its own and bolted from Gorbachev's control.

The ferment of reform meanwhile was spreading throughout Eastern Europe. Gorbachev was unwilling to shoulder the cost of further propping up unpopular satellite regimes, which the struggling Soviet Union could not afford. He also was well aware that continuing to do so would destroy his policy of normalizing relations with the West. That is why in 1989 he warned the regimes of Eastern Europe that they would have to introduce reforms or risk being swept away. Gorbachev hoped that they could revitalize socialism in Eastern Europe. Instead, beginning in mid-year in Poland and Hungary, the Communist regimes began to splinter and collapse. It was at this point that Gorbachev faced a historic choice: use force to save Communism in Eastern Europe, and destroy both his new foreign policy and his reform program at home in the process, or accept the demise of the regimes Stalin had imposed over four decades earlier. Gorbachev, to his great credit, chose the second course. During the summer of 1989 he publicly repudiated the Brezhnev Doctrine under which the Soviet Union had maintained the right to intervene abroad to save Communist regimes. In effect it was replaced by what one Soviet official dubbed the "Sinatra Doctrine": henceforth the Eastern European states would "do it their way." By the end of the year the continental Communist collapse had swept from Poland and Hungary to East Germany, Bulgaria, Czechoslovakia, and Romania. The symbolic climax occurred on November 9, when the crumbling Communist regime in East Germany, in a last futile attempt to survive, opened the Berlin Wall. Tens of thousands of Germans from east and west celebrated freedom around and on the hated structure that for twenty-eight years had stood for oppression, the division of Europe, and the Cold War itself. As 1990 dawned, the only former Eastern European satellite still under Communist rule was tiny and isolated Albania, an ultra hard-line, lone-wolf state whose leadership had broken with the Soviet Union back in the 1960s.

The Cold War Ends

By 1989 announcements from some quarters, ranging from the *New York Times* to Mikhail Gorbachev, were heralding the end of the Cold War. Something approaching an official declaration took place in 1990. During that year several agreements helped close the book on the Cold War, beginning with Soviet commitments to Hungary and Czechoslovakia to withdraw its troops from those two former satellites. In June, Gorbachev came to Washington for a summit meeting with George Bush in which the two leaders signed agreements dealing with both chemical and nuclear weapons. Perhaps most significantly, during the fall of 1990 the question of German unification was resolved. The settlement took place on Western, and especially German, terms not Soviet ones. There was, in fact, no great enthusiasm in the West for immediate German reunification, but both Western hesitancy and Soviet opposition were unable to derail the blitzkrieg diplomatic campaign launched by German chancellor Helmut Kohl, who lavished assurances about German peaceful intentions on leaders from Washington to Moscow. After holding out for a while, Gorbachev accepted both German reunification and its membership in NATO. In return he received limits on the size of the German army, Germany's renunciation of nuclear, chemical, and biological weapons, a guarantee that NATO troops would not be stationed on the territory of the former East Germany, and billions of dollars of desperately needed aid. Germany's official reunification took place on October 3, erasing yet another of the most indelible marks of the Cold War. Twelve days later Mikhail Gorbachev was awarded the Nobel Peace Prize for 1990, an honor he richly deserved.

On November 21, 1990, the United States, the Soviet Union, and thirty other nations signed the Charter of Paris, a document designed to regulate their relations in the post–Cold War era. The charter included a nonaggression pact between NATO and the soon-to-be-dissolved Warsaw Pact. After signing the charter, President George Bush provided a low-key, semiofficial epitaph to the long, bitter, and costly struggle that had dominated world affairs since 1945 when he said, "We have closed a chapter in history. The Cold War is over."

That point was underscored by a major arms agreement reducing conventional forces in Europe, the Conventional Forces in Europe (CFE) treaty, signed in Paris two days earlier. The Cold War's passing was further demonstrated in early 1991 by Soviet acquiescence to Operation Desert Storm. In that American-led military campaign, a coalition of nations drove Iraq, which had invaded Kuwait in August 1990, from its small oil-rich neighbor. The signing in July of the START I treaty, which called for major cuts in the superpowers' nuclear arsenals, was an important step out of the Cold War's long nuclear shadow.

What Factors Decided and Ultimately Ended the Cold War?

The policy of containment and what it did or did not achieve remains a matter of debate among historians of the Cold War. Revisionist historians continue to view it as an overreaction to Soviet activities which, they believe, were not a threat to American security. Revisionists see containment as a policy that inevitably led the United States to prop up undemocratic regimes throughout the world and to a series of harmful blunders, the worst of which was the quagmire of Vietnam.

However, although at times the United States did overreact and, as containment became global in scope, failed to distinguish between vital and secondary interests, the case for containment as being both necessary and successful appears to be quite solid. There is substantial evidence that immediately after World War II a real threat existed to Western Europe, and hence to democratic political systems and America's vital national interests. The Soviet Union was not simply another authoritarian regime; it was a totalitarian society led by Joseph Stalin, a paranoid and ruthless dictator who viewed the Communist and capitalist worlds as irreconcilable enemies.

Documentable Soviet expansionist designs, combined with weakness and demoralization in Western Europe, could have led to Communist takeovers and therefore destroyed democracy in countries like France and Italy, even without direct Soviet intervention. Containment restored the shattered balance of power in Europe and within a short time enabled the democratic societies of the West to recover. As historians John Spanier and Steven W. Hook have put it, after the defeat of Nazi Germany in World War II, containment facilitated the "defeat of the second totalitarian challenge to Western-style democracy" in the twentieth century.[2] Over the long run and despite excesses and blunders that were a part of containment, the policy also forced a change in Soviet society that in fact led to its dissolution, much as George F. Kennan predicted back in 1947.

The Role of Nuclear Weapons

The role of nuclear weapons in determining the shape and duration of the Cold War is another issue that divides historians. Richard Ned Lebow and Janice Gross Stein argue that the Soviet and American policies of deterrence based on nuclear weapons "provoked the type of behavior it was designed to prevent" and in fact "likely prolonged the Cold War."[3] However, there is a persuasive case nuclear weapons, whose use by the superpowers would have destroyed civilization, preserved the peace until the Cold War could be resolved. John Lewis Gaddis has written that "what we wound up doing with nuclear weapons was buying time." Arthur Schlesinger has observed that nuclear weapons were the "reason the Cold War never exploded into a hot war" and therefore suggested with a touch of irony that "the Nobel peace prize should have gone to the atomic bomb." Along the same lines, Thomas Powers answered the question of who "won" the Cold War by observing, "The bomb won."[4]

If it can be persuasively argued that the awesome power of atomic weapons kept the Cold War within limits, another type of power without any physical qualities whatsoever played a pivotal role in tilting the scales toward the West: the power of ideas. Since 1985 it has become increasingly clear just how important American support for the ideas of democracy, freedom, and human rights was to dissidents living behind the Iron Curtain, who listened to American broadcasts on the Voice of America and Radio Liberty and took heart from the Helsinki Accords. The accords in particular served as morale boosters for dissident organizations such as Charter 77 in Czechoslovakia, Solidarity in Poland, and human rights groups in the Soviet Union, where the accords served, in Martin Walker's words, as "the West's secret weapon, a time bomb planted in the heart of the Soviet empire."[5] In short, during the course of the Cold War the United States provided crucial support for advocates of democracy on both sides of the Iron Curtain.

The Cold War finally ended when the Soviet Union became economically exhausted by the burdens of keeping up with the far richer and more efficient United States and its allies. Yet it has often been pointed out that even an exhausted Soviet Union probably would have continued the struggle if its post-Brezhnev leadership had remained within the traditional Soviet mold. Thus, along with economic exhaustion, the advent of Mikhail Gorbachev and his path-breaking policy of perestroika was another necessary factor in ending the Cold War.

What Were the Costs of the Cold War?

Losers, winners, and even nonparticipants all paid a heavy price for the Cold War. The burden of the Cold War severely weakened the Soviet Union and prepared the way for its demise in December 1991. The United States, the supposedly victorious superpower, also paid dearly for the Cold War. It forced America to pour resources into the military that were needed for civilian uses. As its civilian infrastructure deteriorated from lack of long-term support, during the 1980s the United States was transformed by its massive budget and balance of payment deficits from the world's largest creditor into the world's largest debtor nation. By 1990 the United States was paying almost a quarter of a trillion dollars interest annually on its skyrocketing national debt. About 15 percent of that money went to foreign bond holders, the majority of whom were Japanese. Many of America's leading high-tech companies focused their resources and scientific expertise on military rather than civilian industrial applications. These factors help explain the difficulty the U.S. companies had by the Cold War's close in competing with German and Japanese industrial firms in civilian industrial markets worldwide, including those in the United States itself.

The Cold War's decades-long unbroken string of huge military budgets promoted what President Eisenhower in his 1961 farewell address called the "military-industrial complex," an interlocking network made up of the federal military establishment and companies producing arms and other defense-related products, all with an interest in maintaining or increasing military expenditures. Eisenhower worried that the military-industrial complex could distort the American economy and undermine the country's economic health. The Cold War certainly distorted the federal government. By the time the Cold War finally ended, as Ernest R. May has noted, the Pentagon was "the crest of a mountainous defense establishment, which employs two-thirds of the nearly five million persons who work for the U.S. government." This establishment, which includes branches concerned with national security, intelligence, foreign affairs, and other agencies designed to enlist broad sectors of American society in what May calls the "global diplomatic-military contest with a hostile, secretive, heavily armed rival superpower," appears, he argues, poorly suited to meeting the challenges the United States faces in the post–Cold War era.[6] In fact, the origins of what some historians call the "national security state" date from World War I. World War II accelerated its development exponentially. But it was the Cold War that made it an integral and enormous part of American life during what at least officially was peacetime.

The American way of life suffered in other ways as the country focused so much of its energy on the Cold War. The United States became a more violent society with a burgeoning prison population. The government's failure to tell the truth about its conduct of the Vietnam War made many Americans cynical about what public officials told them. The Watergate scandal widened a breach between the American people and their government that, for many, did not close in subsequent decades. Yet it is also true that as the Cold War ended the influence of American culture worldwide was greater than ever before. American blue jeans, rock & roll, and fast-food outlets seemed to be everywhere. Potentially much more important, as historian Warren I. Cohen has pointed out, was the heightened international "concern for human rights, the hope for governments that rule by law—governments of the people, for the people, by the people—and the illusions about the miracles that a market economy will bring."[7]

Beyond the borders of the Cold War participants, the costs of that struggle also could be measured in the neglect of serious and worsening problems, from environmental deterioration to ethnic conflicts that wreaked havoc in many regions, including in some of the world's poorest countries. The end of the Cold War created the opportunity to devote more time and resources to those problems, but by itself did not assure that the necessary commitment would be mustered to combat them.

1. See Samuel F. Wells, "Nuclear Weapons and European Security During the Cold War," in Michael J. Hogan, ed., *The End of the Cold War* (New York: Cambridge University Press, 1992), and Raymond L. Garthoff, *The Great Transition: American-Soviet Relations and the End of the Cold War* (Washington, D.C.: Brookings Institution, 1994). For a journalistic overview of "the turn" from Cold War to "a new era" see Don Oberdorfer, *The Turn: From the Cold War to a New Era, the United States and the Soviet Union, 1983–1990* (New York: Poseidon Press, 1991). Oberdorfer is a foreign affairs correspondent for the *Washington Post*.

2. John Spanier, *American Foreign Policy Since World War II*, 13th ed. (Washington, D.C.: CQ Press, 1995), p. 253.

3. Richard Ned Lebow and Janice Gross Stein, *We All Lost the Cold War* (Princeton: Princeton University Press, 1994), pp. 368, 376.

4. See John Lewis Gaddis, "The Cold War, the Long Peace, and the Future," p. 30; Arthur Schlesinger, "Some Lessons from the Cold War," p. 54; Thomas Powers, "Who Won the Cold War?" p. 27.

5. Martin Walker, *The Cold War: A History* (New York: Henry Holt, 1993), p. 237.

6. Ernest R. May, "The U.S. Government, a Legacy of the Cold War," in Michael Hogan, ed., *The End of the Cold War: Its Meaning and Implications* (New York: Cambridge University Press, 1992), p. 217.

7. Warren I. Cohen, *The Cambridge History of American Foreign Relations* vol. IV, *America in the Age of Soviet Power, 1945–1991* (New York: Cambridge University Press, 1993), p. 259.

CHAPTER 3

Science and Society

AMERICA'S DECADES

The Discovery of a "Gay Disease"

Steven Epstein

In the essay that follows, Steven Epstein, a professor of sociology at the University of California, San Diego, traces the first incidents of AIDS and doctors' and the general public's initial reactions to the strange new disease. Because in the United States many of the first victims of the disease were homosexual men, explains Epstein, the medical community, and much of the general public, assumed the disease must be caused by some aspect of the gay lifestyle. Doctors referred to the condition as "the gay cancer" and Gay-Related Immune Deficiency. However, in 1982, as reports of heterosexuals with the condition became more widely publicized, scientists renamed the disease AIDS. Finally in 1983, when several hemophiliacs reported symptoms after receiving blood transfusions, many in the medical community became convinced that the cause of AIDS was actually a blood-borne virus (later isolated and named HIV) rather than a direct result of intravenous drug use or sexual activity.

When a puzzling new medical syndrome was first reported to be afflicting—and killing—young gay men in certain cities in the United States, there was no particular reason to expect that the cause might be a previously unknown virus. Nor did the deaths immediately take on any

---

great medical significance. Michael Gottlieb, a young im-munologist at the teaching hospital of the University of Cal-ifornia at Los Angeles, began seeing such cases in late 1980 but found that he couldn't spark the interest of the *New En-gland Journal of Medicine,* the most prestigious medical journal in the country, later to publish hundreds of articles on AIDS. In early 1981 the *New England Journal*'s editor instead referred Gottlieb to the U.S. Centers for Disease Control (CDC), the federal agency in Atlanta, Georgia, re-sponsible for tracking diseases and controlling their spread.

"Gay Cancer"

The CDC's first report, published in its *Morbidity and Mortality Weekly Report* in June 1981, noted only that five young men in Los Angeles, "all active homosexuals," had been treated over the course of the past year for *Pneumo-cystis carinii* pneumonia (PCP). Two of the men had died. The microorganism that causes PCP is ubiquitous but is normally kept easily at bay by the body's immune system; therefore cases of PCP were exceedingly rare, restricted to people who were immunosuppressed because of medical treatment (such as chemotherapy) or who for other reasons had severely malfunctioning immune systems. The CDC re-port zeroed in on the question of sexuality—"the fact that these patients were all homosexual"—to put forward two tentative hypotheses: that the PCP outbreak was associated with "some aspect of a homosexual lifestyle" or with "dis-ease acquired through sexual contact." However, "the pa-tients did not know each other and had no known common contacts or knowledge of sexual partners who had had similar illnesses."

A few weeks later, the CDC reported twenty-six cases (twenty in New York City and six in California) of young homosexual men suffering from Kaposi's sarcoma, a rare form of cancer normally found in elderly men. At least four of the men also had cases of PCP; eight of them had died. On the basis of this report, Dr. Lawrence Altman, medical reporter for the *New York Times,* wrote a short article about the cases of cancer in homosexuals. Appearing deep inside the newspaper on page A-20, the article sounded what would become one of the most common themes in mainstream media coverage of the epidemic: "The reporting doctors said that most cases had involved homosexual men who have had multiple and frequent sexual encounters with different partners, as many as ten sexual encounters each night up to four times a week." Soon after, Dr. Lawrence Mass, health writer for the *New York Native*— the most widely read gay newspaper in New York City and one of only a few to have a national readership—also addressed the question of promiscuity. In an article about "Cancer in the Gay Community," Mass wrote: "At this time, many feel that sexual frequency with a multiplicity of partners—what some would call promiscuity—is the single overriding risk factor. . . ."

Mass's article also explored a range of possible explanations for what he called (in quotes) "the gay cancer," including "an infectious or otherwise cancerous agent," but he noted that the "current consensus of informed opinion is that multiple factors are involved in the present outbreak of Kaposi's sarcoma among gay males." He quoted Dr. Donna Mildvan, chief of infectious diseases at Beth Israel Medical Center, who reported a colleague's belief that the outbreak of illnesses "has to do with the bombardment, the clustering of a whole range of infectious diseases among these patients which may be exhausting their immunodefensive capacities." And he cited Dr. Alvin Friedman-Kien, a professor of dermatology and microbiology at New York University Medical Center, who had examined some of the Kaposi's sarcoma patients and who had speculated about the possible role of amyl nitrite or butyl nitrite inhalants. These inhalants, street drugs that were sold legally and were popular in gay male communities at the time, were often called "poppers" because consumers would pop open the packaging to release the fumes, which were then inhaled to produce a "rush" or to intensify orgasm. Nitrites were believed to have immunosuppressive effects. On the other hand, they had been prescribed to cardiac patients for years, and no unusual cases of PCP or Kaposi's sarcoma had ever been reported in that population.

The "Immune Overload" Hypothesis

By the beginning of 1982, a series of more detailed reports in medical journals such as the *New England Journal* was available as a source of additional information and speculation for researchers and medical practitioners, and for translation into the media, particularly the gay press. Researchers agreed that the telltale marker of these cases of immunosuppression was a deficiency in the numbers of "helper T cells"—or in other accounts, an abnormal ratio of helper T cells to suppressor T cells—types of white blood cells involved in the body's immune response. But questions of etiology and epidemiology were considerably more confusing. For one thing, it was already apparent that the "nationwide epidemic of immunodeficiency among male homosexuals" was in fact not restricted to gay men. According to the CDC's task force on the syndrome, 8 percent of the 159 cases were among heterosexuals, one of whom was a woman. In the pages of the *New England Journal*, Michael Gottlieb and his coauthors, the Los Angeles clinicians who had first reported the syndrome to the CDC, described finding the same syndrome in two exclusively heterosexual men, while Henry Masur and coauthors reported eleven cases of PCP in the New York area—five injection drug users, four gay men, and two men who were both.

Nonetheless, the focus of attention in all the medical literature remained squarely on the male homosexual sufferers, as evidenced by descriptors such as Brennan and Durack's "Gay Compromise Syndrome" and Masur et al.'s more euphemistic "Community-Acquired *Pneumocystis Carinii* Pneumonia." All speculation about causes proceeded from the premise of the centrality of male homosexuality. In Durack's words: "What clue does the link with homosexuality provide? Homosexual men, especially those

The Reality of AIDS Shocks America

The announcement in August 1985 that movie-idol Rock Hudson, who had been a romantic symbol for millions, was dying of AIDS did more than any other single event to shock the public into realization that this disease is a deadly threat that can affect anyone. Even President Ronald Reagan did not fully grasp the seriousness of the epidemic until he heard the news about his old friend. On October 3, 1985, the day of Hudson's death, the House of Representatives nearly doubled the funds appropriated for AIDS research, to $189 million, and on the following day the Senate Appropriations Committee raised the total of AIDS funding to $221 million. . . .

Public awareness of the AIDS problem was expanded further as the disease became a popular theme in fictional dramas. Two hit plays, *As Is* and *The Normal Heart,* featured sensitive treatments of the loves and trials of men dying with AIDS. A segment of the *Trapper John* TV series dealt with the dilemmas of a hospital treating an AIDS patient. The disease even found its way into a sitcom: An episode of the Showtime series *Brothers* began with the studio audience laughing at one-liners and ended in stunned silence as characters grappled with questions like "How do you deal with the fact that death comes from loving?" *An Early Frost,* a TV movie about a young lawyer with AIDS, won critical acclaim and stirred intense interest among nearly fifty million viewers all over the United States. The leading characters of the AIDS dramas were gay men, but the stories were presented as broader human problems affecting everyone.

Just a few years later, it seems hard to remember how shocking those early AIDS dramas were. AIDS has become a part of the background of daily life for Americans, even those who have had no direct personal contact with the disease.

Alvin and Virginia Silverstein, *AIDS: Deadly Threat.* Hillside, NJ: Enslow, 1991.

who have many partners, are more likely than the general population to contract sexually transmitted diseases. Lesbians are not, and this apparent freedom, whatever its explanation, seems to extend to Kaposi's sarcoma and opportunistic infections." Yet the assumption that the syndrome was somehow linked with homosexuality actually did little to immediately clarify the etiology, as Durack and others realized. Noting that "male homosexuals are at increased risk for the acquisition of common viral infections" such as cytomegalovirus (CMV), hepatitis B, and Epstein-Barr virus, Durack described the "obvious problem" with the hypothesis that CMV, or any of these viruses, might be the cause: "It does not explain why this syndrome is apparently new. Homosexuality is at least as old as history, and cytomegalovirus is presumably not a new pathogen. Were the homosexual contemporaries of Plato, Michelangelo, and Oscar Wilde subject to the risk of dying from opportunistic infections?" Durack's supposition was that "some new factor," such as poppers, "may have distorted the host-parasite relationship." Concluding with some "frank speculation," Durack put forward a model essentially identical to the one Mildvan had proposed to the *Native:* that "the combined effects of persistent viral infection plus an adjuvant drug cause immunosuppression in some genetically predisposed men."

This model, which was sometimes called the "immune overload" or "antigen overload" hypothesis, represented the initial medical frame for understanding the epidemic: the syndrome was essentially linked to gay men, specifically to the "excesses" of the "homosexual lifestyle." The epidemic coincided historically, *Newsweek* suggested in the article "Diseases That Plague Gays," "with the burgeoning of bathhouses, gay bars and bookstores in major cities where homosexual men meet." Urban gay men, enjoying "life in the fast lane," had subjected themselves to so many sexually transmitted diseases, taken so many strong treatments to fight those diseases, and done so many recreational drugs that their immune systems had ultimately given up altogether, leaving their bodies open to the on-slaught of a range of opportunistic infections. As one Harvard doctor is reported to have put it informally, "overindulgence in sex and drugs" and "the New York City lifestyle" were the culprits. What distinguished gay men from CMV-infected, sexually adventurous heterosexuals, and from cardiac patients inhaling amyl nitrite, and from the many patients who took strong antibiotic or antiparasitic drugs was, these experts suggested, that only gay men (or those gay men living in the "fast lane") confronted all these risks at once. . . .

From "GRID" to AIDS

With the advantage of hindsight, it is easy to recognize that the initial link between gay men and the new syndrome—while certainly the single most consequential aspect of the social construction of the epidemic—in fact reflected the confounding influences of what Irving Zola has called the "pathways" from doctor to patient. . . .

To put it simply, some people get better medical attention, which means that medical professionals "attend" to their "unique" conditions. In New York City, if not elsewhere, it appears likely that there were at least as many cases of pneumocystis pneumonia among injection drug users as among gay men at the time of the discovery of the syndrome. But gay men, some of them affluent and relatively privileged, found their way into private doctors' offices and prominent teaching hospitals—and from there into the pages of medical journals—while drug users often sickened and died with little fanfare. Even as cases among injection drug users began to be reported, the "gay disease" frame for understanding the epidemic was already falling into place. Colloquially, the epidemic became known among some medical professionals and researchers in early 1982 as "GRID": Gay-Related Immune Deficiency. . . .

Sensitive to the fact that gay doctors and activists criticized the informal "GRID" designation, the CDC came up with an official name for the epidemic in May 1982 and first used the term in print in September of that year. This name was chosen specifically for its neutrality—Acquired Immunodeficiency Syndrome, or AIDS: "acquired" to distinguish it from congenital defects of the immune system; "immunodeficiency" to describe the underlying problem, the deterioration of immune system functioning (and specifically, a decline in the numbers of helper T cells, causing the body to lose most of its capacity to ward off infection); and "syndrome" to indicate that the condition was not a disease in itself, but rather was marked by the presence of some other, relatively uncommon disease or infection (like PCP or Kaposi's sarcoma), "occurring in a person with no known cause for diminished resistance to that disease." This was strictly a "surveillance" definition, for epidemiological reporting purposes: it did not imply any knowledge about what AIDS "really was." But in the absence of a lab test for a known cause, this definition at least allowed the CDC a crude measure of the scope of the problem.

New Cases of AIDS in the United States, 1985

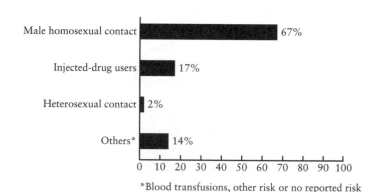

*Blood transfusions, other risk or no reported risk

Source: National Institutes of Health.

The newly defined syndrome would, over the course of 1983, achieve the status of a "Worldwide Health Problem," as the headline of one of Lawrence Altman's articles in the *New York Times* labeled it in November. By that time, AIDS cases would be reported "in 33 countries and all inhabited continents." Though most cases were in the United States or Europe, the most striking aspect of the epidemic's spread was the discovery of AIDS in equatorial Africa. In April the *Washington Post* summarized reports appearing in both *Lancet* and the *New England Journal* that described cases of AIDS in European countries, but among patients who had immigrated from or traveled in countries such as Zaire and Chad. Of twenty-nine such cases in France, six patients had become ill before June 1981—that is, before the epidemic was first reported in the United States. Immediately scientists and reporters in the West picked up on the notion that Africa "could have been the breeding place" for the epidemic.

Despite the globalization of the epidemic and the formal change in terminology, the "gay disease" formulation, in various guises, continued to undergird medical investigation of the syndrome through the first half of 1982. For example, an editorial in the *Annals of Internal Medicine* by Dr. Anthony Fauci, a distinguished scientist who would later become the head of the AIDS program at the National Institutes of Health (NIH), laid out a number of etiological possibilities: "Is there a new virus or other infectious agent that has expressed itself first among the male homosexual community because of the unusual exposure potential within this group? Is this an immunosuppressed state due to chronic exposure to a recognized virus or viruses? Is this illness due to a synergy among various factors such as infectious agents, recreational drugs, therapeutic agents administered for diseases that are peculiar to this population such as the 'gay bowel syndrome'. . . ?" But what Fauci never doubted was that the "critical questions" were: "why homosexual men and why occurrence or recognition only as recently as 1979?"

A Virus Causes AIDS

Suddenly, this whole framework for understanding the epidemic was dramatically challenged. On July 9, the CDC reported thirty-four cases of Kaposi's sarcoma or opportunistic infections among Haitians living in five different states in the United States. None of those interviewed reported homosexual activity, and only one gave a history of injection drug use. The following week the agency reported three cases of PCP in people with hemophilia, all of them recipients of a blood product called Factor VIII, "manufactured from plasma pools collected from as many as a thousand or more donors." The CDC refrained from drawing conclusions, but noted that the occurrence of the hemophilia cases "suggests the possible transmission of an agent through blood products." Since bacteria were screened out of Factor VIII in the production process, while smaller particles such as viruses could potentially escape the screen, the "agent" in question would almost certainly have to be a virus.

Mass, writing in the *Native,* quickly noted the significance of these findings: of all the existing etiological hypotheses, "only that of viruses would seem able to provide a unitary hypothesis that could explain the sudden appearance of AID [the *Native*'s term at that time] in a growing number of distinct populations.". . .

Once put squarely on the table, the notion of a single, unifying cause of AIDS carried with it immediate practical implications. The virus theory, now described by the *Los Angeles Times* as "a potentially much more serious candidate for the cause," was also a scary one, as it "raised the specter" of a communicable disease that might potentially affect anyone. Or as *Newsweek* warned in August, "the 'homosexual plague' has started spilling over into the general population." With the news, toward the end of 1982, of a case of AIDS having developed in a blood transfusion recipient twenty months old (one of whose donors was found to have AIDS) and of other cases in the female sexual partners of intravenous drug users with AIDS, the viral hypothesis gained increasing credibility.

The War on Drugs

Michael Schaller

In the following excerpt from his book *Reckoning with Reagan: America and Its President in the 1980s*, Michael Schaller describes the antidrug efforts of the mid- to late 1980s. In Reagan's second term, in reaction to what opinion polls indicated was an epidemic of drug use, the president declared drug trafficking a threat to national security and increased funding for drug control efforts, and he and Nancy Reagan launched a "just say no" campaign intended to discourage young people from using drugs. Schaller, a professor of history at the University of Arizona, points out that hysteria over drugs increased just as the Cold War was coming to an end; he suggests that, in the minds of many Americans, drug abuse replaced communism as America's greatest enemy.

A merican presidents, starting with Woodrow Wilson, have declared a series of wars on drugs. The federal role began with the passage of the Harrison Act in 1916, which banned opiates and classified drug users as criminals. A New Deal law of 1937 made marijuana use a federal crime. Laws passed during the Truman, Eisenhower, and Nixon administrations broadened the penalties against drug use and criminalized a wider variety of natural and synthetic substances. Nixon replaced the Narcotics Bureau

Excerpted from *Reckoning with Reagan: America and Its President in the 1980s,* by Michael Schaller. Copyright ©1992 by Oxford University Press, Inc. Reprinted with permission from Oxford University Press, Inc.

with a more powerful Drug Enforcement Administration, and Reagan bolstered the DEA further. Narcotics laws sent many people to jail but had little impact on the problem. The use of opiates, marijuana, and other psychoactive drugs waxed and waned in a rhythm of its own.

The American approach to drug control had long relied on three weapons: (1) the eradication of opium poppies, marijuana, and coca leaf at its foreign source (Turkey, Peru, Southeast Asia, for example); (2) the interdiction of drugs as they entered the United States; and (3) vigorous police efforts to arrest drug dealers and users in the local community. Ever since 1916 these efforts had been highly politicized and dismal failures.

Historically, drug-use patterns are difficult to predict or understand. However, in many cases the use of psychoactive substances such as heroin, marijuana, and cocaine have tended to run in cycles. A new drug is introduced, finds a following, experiences a surge in use for five to ten years, and then declines in popularity when the user community sees its dangerous effects. During the 1950s heroin use rose and declined, marijuana was in vogue from the middle 1960s through the late 1970s, and cocaine use escalated during the second half of the 1970s. This generalization must also take into account varying levels of drug use among different economic classes and ethnic and minority groups.

Just Say No

In 1985, 1% of Americans surveyed listed drugs as a major threat to the nation. By 1989, more than half the population described drug use as a grave threat to national security. President and Mrs. Reagan, declaring that the nation faced an unprecedented epidemic of drug use, urged even stricter criminal penalties and implored the public to "just say no." When Reagan left office, federal, state, and local authorities were spending about $15 billion annually to fight a "war on drugs." Three-fourths of the money went to law enforcement and incarceration. Drug offenders constituted the fastest growing sector of the prison population.

The Reagan anti-drug crusade coincided with the reduction of tension with the Soviet Union during the president's second term. To an extent, the drug war replaced the Cold War while "narco-terrorism" replaced the Red Army as public enemy #1. This "militarization" of drug policy found expression in a National Security Council directive Reagan approved in 1986, calling drug traffic a threat to the security of the United States and the entire Western hemisphere. Just as the Chinese Communists had been blamed during the 1950s for the surge in heroin addiction, Reagan accused communist governments in Cuba and Nicaragua of abetting cocaine imports. . . .

The public tended to ignore the foreign policy implications of the Reagan anti-drug campaign but did respond to individual tragedy. The 1986 death from cocaine overdose of Len Bias, a promising basketball player at the University of Maryland who had just signed a lucrative professional contract, became a major national news event. Journalists and public officials asked, plaintively, why an athlete with such promise used cocaine. Few questioned how he had reached his senior year despite failing most of his courses.

Ronald and Nancy Reagan denounced drug use as immoral and reaffirmed their belief that religion, school discipline, and harsh criminal penalties were the best antidote. Whether true or not, the Reagan's definition of norms varied dramatically from the real behavior of Americans. Each year during the 1980s, an estimated 40 million people (about one in six) consumed an illegal substance. A 1987 survey revealed that half of all citizens under age 45 had smoked marijuana at least once in their life. Almost three-quarters of a million Americans faced drug charges each year in the 1980s, mostly for possession of marijuana.

In spite of the hysteria about increasing drug use, accurate statistics were hard to come by. Local police stepped up enforcement of narcotic laws when the issue gained prominence. Police departments also learned that they could secure larger budgets by stressing the drug problem. Impartial experts believe that drug use among non-minorities and the middle class probably peaked at the end of the 1970s and actually declined during the 1980s.

A Rise in Cocaine Use and Drug-Related Violence

In contrast, use of cocaine and its derivatives, like crack, grew in popularity among the urban poor and minority youth. For some, staying high relieved the miseries of daily life. Others found selling drugs provided one of the few avenues of economic and social mobility. The effects on individual, family, and community life were tragic. But the response of government at all levels—putting more drug users in jail—basically ignored the tragedy. While the social stigma and physical trauma of mandatory jail time probably deterred many middle-class youth from using drugs, it had little impact on inner-city minorities who often found a year or two of incarceration an improvement on their normal living conditions.

The federal government and media seldom discussed the root causes of drug use and often misrepresented its physical consequences. Narcotics killed relatively few drug users—about 4,000 to 5,000 in a typical year during the 1980s. America's legal drugs of choice—alcohol and tobacco—killed 200 to 300 times as many people. For example, alcohol-related deaths approached 200,000 annually while tobacco killed over 300,000 Americans each year. Violent turf wars among drug dealers and robberies to raise money for drug buys killed twice as many people—about 8,000 annually—as narcotics did directly.

Nancy Reagan first visited a crisis nursery for children of drug addicts in 1984. She delivered a speech written by Peggy Noonan, whom she had neither met nor discussed the subject with. "The things I've seen," she told reporters (in Noonan's words), "would make the strongest heart break." She and the president repeated these visits several times over the next four years.

President Reagan, like most citizens, was more troubled

by the escalation of drug-related violence than with the question of why youths used drugs or how to rehabilitate addicts. The aggressive behavior associated with smoking "crack" cocaine seemed especially worrisome. The Drug Enforcement Administration focused anti-drug efforts on the dramatic but largely futile campaign to interdict supplies, arrest dealers, and jail users. For example, Reagan placed Vice President George Bush in charge of a task force to halt drug smuggling into Florida. Predictably, less drugs entered Florida, as smugglers shifted operations elsewhere.

The Drug Enforcement Administration and local authorities measured success in the tonnage of drugs seized and the numbers of smugglers arrested. Since the cost of producing and transporting drugs represented a small portion of eventual profits, interdiction hardly made a dent in the incentive to smuggle. Perhaps because therapy programs were much less telegenic than car and boat chases, only about one-fourth of the money expended on the drug problem and little attention went into drug education or rehabilitation.

Dubious Victory in the Drug War

In his enthusiasm to suppress drugs, President Reagan urged compulsory urine tests—chemical loyalty oaths, as civil libertarians called them—of millions of workers who showed no evidence of abuse. In many cases, courts permitted this. By 1989, state and federal prisons were bursting with drug felons sentenced to long mandatory terms but cocaine was as available as before. Police began reporting decreased levels of cocaine use in 1990. Predictably, authorities claimed success. However, as with earlier drug epidemics, the "consumer product cycle," rather than legal sanctions, played a large role. Many addicts and casual users seemed to have switched brands, often to a new generation of synthetic drugs or to an old standby, heroin. Polling data suggested that the public had begun turning its attention in other directions. In any case, during the 1980s, as before, alcohol remained the drug most abused by all sectors of American society.

The Personal Computer Revolution

Karl T. Thurber Jr.

The prototype for the modern computer was ENIAC (Electronic Numerical Integrator and Calculator), a huge, 30-ton machine built in 1946. It took several breakthroughs in electronics—the invention of the transistor, the integrated circuit, and the silicon microchip—before computers became small enough for personal use.

But computers did become smaller and more affordable, as writer Karl T. Thurber Jr. explains in the following article from *Popular Electronics* magazine. Personal computers (PCs) first became popular among computer hobbyists and some businesses in the 1970s. However, most observers agree that the "PC revolution" truly began in 1981, with the release of the IBM PC. As the 1980s wore on, personal computers could increasingly be found in homes, schools, and offices. The PC revolution of the 1980s would eventually give way to the rise of the Internet and the information revolution of the 1990s.

To many, the 1960's were the glory days of the computer revolution. In that era, large computers—the heavyweight, solid-state, big-business descendants of ENIAC, MANIAC, BINAC, UNIVAC, and the like, occupied whole floors or even buildings of universities and businesses. Mid-century America was full of big computers years before

Excerpted from "Buried Bytes: A History of the Personal Computer," by Karl T. Thurber Jr., *Popular Electronics,* April 1995. Reprinted with permission from Gernsback Publications, Inc.

anyone even dreamed of calling them "personal." After all, no one but a tinkerer or an egomaniac would want a computer occupying every last square inch of his or her office, let alone having one that might noticeably sag his or her desk with its weight. But things were about to change.

The PC Industry's Incubation

It turned out that in the 1960's and 1970's, there were a few visionaries who wanted desktop computer power they could control themselves. They wanted to forever dispense with the isolation, elitism, and centralized control associated with the large computers, called mainframes. Those early hackers and technoids who influenced the development of the PC predate what we'll call the 1970's PC incubator. At the outset, those PC enthusiasts were mainframe and minicomputer hobbyists.

Hobbyist interest in computers can be traced back at least to the 1960's when Digital Equipment Corp. (DEC) introduced its PDP series minicomputer, particularly the "relatively inexpensive" ($24,000) PDP-8 mini. Also, in the mid-1960's, the ad hoc Midnight Computer Wiring Society of MIT (Massachusetts Institute of Technology) took shape. It was spontaneously and nocturnally convened when the current crop of young hackers needed to creatively work around MIT's extensive regulations against unauthorized tampering with its valuable digital computers.

What was emerging at MIT, Stanford, and other academic institutions with their bright computer-science students is often referred to as the Hacker Ethic. That ethic states, among other things, that access to computers should be unlimited and total, information should be free to all, centralized authority is to be mistrusted, and computers are good in that they can change your life for the better. That ethic, which is still alive today in one form or another, is much better suited to the PC than it is to the mainframe or mini.

While all of that was going on, microchip technology continued to evolve. One of the most important steps in that evolution occurred in 1971 when an American engineer, Ted Hoff, placed the essential elements of a computer on one silicon chip, which he called a microprocessor. The Intel 4004 and the many CPU- (central-processing unit) chip variations that followed it, are actually the "kernels" that have operated untold millions of modern products and formed the brains of almost every general-purpose electronic computer.

Because the chip-sized CPU represented the very heart of a digital computer, computer hobbyists quickly realized that it was just a matter of time before computers would become affordable to the average guy or gal. That realization helped spawn one of the earliest computer-user's groups—the Homebrew Computer Club of Menlo Park.

Homebrew was formed in 1975 to exchange information, swap ideas, and work on projects related to computers, terminals, and various other digital devices. The club's real significance was that its pioneering, basement- and garage-tinkering, hacker-oriented members strongly influenced the development of the PC on the West Coast. Homebrew also encouraged the formation of similar clubs around the country.

Between the efforts of hackers and the technological developments of the time, the stage was set for computers to indeed become much smaller and reside where an individual could control them, right on his or her desk or workbench. Let's take a look at some of the small "microcomputers" that emerged as a result in the 1970's.

A Revolution Begins

By the mid-1970's, the microprocessor and other integrated circuits had dramatically reduced the cost of the electronic components required in a computer. The first affordable desktop computer specifically for personal use was the Altair 8800, sold by Micro Instrumentation Telemetry Systems (MITS) of Albuquerque, New Mexico.

The MITS Altair 8800 was the microcomputer that hardware hackers loved. Some consider it to be the first commercially available microcomputer, the one that truly kicked off the microcomputer revolution. Even though the Altair was advertised as a minicomputer kit; today we would call it a microcomputer. The term "PC" hadn't caught on just yet. . . .

The Altair never became a commercially suitable computing appliance. For a user to end up with an 8K BASIC-speaking computer, he or she would have to spend nearly $2000 in add-ons for the machine. But the Altair did give

The Apple Macintosh and Microsoft Windows

Among those who looked at the IBM PC and asked why not something better were a group of people at Apple. . . .

In January 1984 Apple introduced the Macintosh in a legendary commercial during the Super Bowl, in which Apple promised that the Macintosh would prevent the year 1984 from being the technological dystopia forecast by Orwell's novel *1984*. The computer sold for $2,495—more than the $1,000 [Apple employee Jef] Raskin was aiming for, but cheaper than the Lisa [Apple's first computer to offer a graphical user interface]. It was more expensive than an IBM PC, but no PC at that time, no matter what software or boards users added, could offer the graphical interface of the Macintosh. . . .

The Mac's elegant system software was its greatest accomplishment. It displayed a combination of aesthetic beauty and practical engineering that is extremely rare. One can point to specific details. When a file was opened or closed, its symbol expanded or contracted on the screen in little steps—somehow it just felt right. Ultimately this feeling is subjective, but it was one that few would disagree with. The Macintosh software was something rarely found among engineering artifacts. The system evolved as the Mac grew, and it was paid the highest compliment from Microsoft, who tried to copy it with its Windows program.

Paul E. Ceruzzi, *A History of Modern Computing*. Cambridge, MA: The Massachusetts Institute of Technology Press, 1998.

a real boost to Bill Gates and Paul Allen, who licensed their version of BASIC to MITS, which enabled the Altair to actually "do something.". . .

Perhaps the Homebrew Computer Club's greatest influence was on the Apple Computer Company of Palo Alto. In 1976, two young computer enthusiasts and Homebrew members, Steve Wozniak and Steve Jobs, began selling a remarkably small and cheap PC, the Apple I, for $666.66. It was based on the brand-new, inexpensive ($20), 8-bit, MOS-Technology 6502 CPU.

Wozniak, known as "the Woz," was a gifted hardware hacker who built the Apple I for his own pleasure and for the enjoyment of his friends, unveiling it in the spring of 1976 at the Homebrew Computer Club. But expecting to actually sell a computer to a nonhacker user was risky business in the mid-1970's. That was a time when gaining acceptance for a PC wasn't an easy task.

Enter Steve Jobs—non-techie visionary, deal-maker, and marketeer. He took the Woz's Apple I and his later Apple II and turned them into real, marketable products. Realizing what a user-friendly and good-looking computer the Apple really was, Jobs made a name for his fledgling company in the industry. The rest, of course, is history. If the Altair kicked off the PC revolution, the Apple defined just what a PC was and ensured that the PC would be a commercial success.

The Apple II wasn't the only hot product around. The Personal Electronic Transactor, or PET, was calculator-maker Commodore International's first computer. Commodore introduced it at the 1977 Consumer Electronics Show in New York. The PET was the brainchild of Chuck Peddle, a gifted engineer who worked for the semiconductor manufacturer, MOS Technology. Commodore, under the leadership of hard-charging entrepreneur Jack Tramiel, presciently acquired MOS Technology to ensure it always had chips available for its use.

The 8-bit, 6502-based PET was quite capable for 1977, being equipped with either a 4K or 8K memory, a built-in green-screen monitor, a tiny keyboard that looked suspiciously like a Commodore calculator keyboard rather than the expected typewriter keyboard, and a built-in cassette recorder for data storage. The PET was priced at a bargain-basement $795, but the backlog for the machines was so great that you had to wait months to get one. . . .

The Commodore PET was, well, just another PC in a new and chaotic industry. But in 1978, Commodore's MOS Technology subsidiary developed a very special chip that let a computer use a color display rather than a black-and-white screen. The Video Interface Chip (VIC), with its colorful 22-column capability, became the impetus for the revolutionary Commodore VIC-20 computer that Commodore introduced in 1981 for under $300.

A consumer could bring the little, one-piece PC home from the local discount store, hook it up to his or her color TV set, and enjoy the computing world in eight glorious colors. No one seemed to mind that it had but 22 columns of rather large and clunky letters as its display, and that it

The invention of small, user-friendly personal computers transformed the home and workplace during the 1980s.

had less than 5K of main-system memory.

The pioneering VIC-20 was followed in 1982 by the legendary Commodore 64, arguably the most popular single computer ever built. The C-64, many thousands of which are still running today, had it all: a 40-column screen, a music-synthesizer chip, easily programmed graphics, and a seemingly infinite 64K RAM.

VIC-20 owners loved the C-64 because they could use their notoriously nonstandard VIC peripherals (disk drives, printers, and modems) with it. The C-64 was initially list-priced at $595, but eventually sold for about one-fourth of that price. In 1983, price cuts and price wars reportedly made Commodore the first personal-computer company to reach $1 billion in sales. . . .

Big Blue and Its Legendary PC

IBM, as the top mainframe outfit, probably didn't want to create anything that might threaten its "big-computer" business. Therefore, it's questionable just how much effort Big Blue really put into developing a PC in 1974, when it produced the $10,000 IBM 5100 desktop and, later, the IBM 5500. Both never went anywhere.

In August 1981, however, IBM, the biggest computer manufacturer, introduced a desktop computer. That lent legitimacy to the concept of the PC, even if IBM wasn't fully committed to its own project and never fully grasped its true significance.

The original 1981 IBM PC used the 8088 CPU—a 16-bit processor in an 8-bit body (because it used a less-technically attractive, 8-bit data bus). The PC came with 64K RAM, one or two 160K floppy-disk drives, and no hard disk; PC-DOS Version 1 didn't support hard disks of any size. That was a big problem, so the IBM PC-XT came out in 1983 with the same 8088 CPU but with 128K RAM, a 360K floppy, and a 10-MB hard disk.

Graphics were optional; the early PC came from the factory only able to display text. Color graphics awaited the development of IBM's Color Graphics Adapter (CGA). In

1984, IBM introduced the then-revolutionary IBM AT (Advanced Technology) PC that used the true 16-bit 80286 CPU. The 80286 was considerably faster and more capable than the 8088.

Many industry observers maintain that IBM has never known what to do with its "little" computers, and much has been written about IBM not properly marketing its own PC's ever since their 1981 introduction. Sadly, IBM's history in the PC business has been marked by failed approaches that focused too heavily on solving its own problems rather then meeting user's needs. Also, IBM let the myriad XT- and AT-clone makers, and the makers of peripheral devices and expansion boards, walk away with most of the hardware profits that might have been IBM's.

One of IBM's biggest failures was its PCjr—a small, stripped-down computer that is remembered today for its spongy, "chiclet-style" keyboard that almost no one liked. The original 1983 model was priced at $669 and didn't sell. IBM was forced to work off its inventory any way it could, and eventually sold the juniors to its own employees for less than cost. IBM's PCjr fiasco brought into serious question whether or not there really was a home-computer market at all.

The company has recently been through some wrenching times. Tens of thousands of IBM employees have lost their jobs and countless investors have seen their stakes shrink. IBM's own market share of PC sales is quite small today as it tries to adapt itself to radically new ways of doing computer business. Only the passage of time will tell if IBM reinvents itself.

We owe a great deal to IBM and its PC. Thanks to IBM's initial decisions and the ability of clone makers to legally reverse-engineer IBM's Basic Input/Output System (BIOS) technology (IBM's BIOS chips themselves were, of course, not for sale), most PC's today are open-architecture systems that help minimize hardware obsolescence and make troubleshooting straightforward.

Before the IBM PC's debut in 1981, the popular machines

of the day—such as the Apple, Tandy TRS-80, Commodore PET, and most others—were largely proprietary, closed systems in which users were locked into buying parts, upgrades, software, and service from the original equipment manufacturer (OEM). Even the external screws on some computers carried dire warnings about users even opening their boxes, much less servicing them. Now you pop your PC's lid without fear. You need have little worry about voiding your warranty, and for that we must thank Big Blue.

Today's personal computer is several hundred times faster than ENIAC, about 3000 times lighter, and millions of dollars cheaper. In rapid succession, computers have shrunk from room-size to tabletop to laptop, and finally to palm size. Personal computers have come a long way since the 1970's, and the PC revolution is still nowhere near complete.

The Space Shuttle *Challenger* Explosion

T.A. Heppenheimer

Since the 1960s, one of the long-term goals of the U.S. space program has been to build a permanently manned space station. However, NASA planners realized that building such a station would require numerous space flights, and that the cost of building rockets for each of these flights would quickly become prohibitive. To overcome this obstacle, NASA began designing the space shuttle, the world's first reusable spacecraft. The shuttle and the station were planned as a single interdependent program.

In the 1980s, the space shuttle became a reality, leading to renewed national interest in the space program. However, as aerospace historian T.A. Heppenheimer explains, confidence in the new spacecraft was shattered on January 28, 1986, when the space shuttle *Challenger* exploded over Cape Kennedy shortly after launch. Heppenheimer discusses the causes of the disaster and the devastating effect it had on NASA and its plans for a manned U.S. space station. Heppenheimer is the author of *Turbulent Skies: The History of Commercial Aviation* and *Countdown: A History of Space Flight*, from which the following essay is excerpted.

Excerpted from *Countdown: A History of Space Flight*, by T.A. Heppenheimer. Copyright ©1997 by T.A. Heppenheimer. Reprinted with permission from John Wiley & Sons, Inc.

NASA had never lost a manned mission. Across fifteen years, in its Mercury, Gemini, Apollo, and Skylab programs, it had a perfect record launching astronauts into space and returning them safely. This bred complacency, as the agency prepared to commit its future to the space-shuttle program. No one expected to see a shuttle explode in the sky over Cape Canaveral; no one anticipated that such a disaster would bring the space program to its knees. . . .

High Hopes for the Space Shuttle

The first flight of the space shuttle took place in April 1981, twenty years from the day when Yuri Gagarin became the first man in space. The shuttle's pilots, John Young and Robert Crippen, faced a very high degree of success-oriented management. The Space Shuttle Main Engine (SSME) had operated only on test stands—never in an actual launch. No preliminary flight had demonstrated that the tiles would stay in place rather than falling off. No astronauts had ever ridden atop solid-fuel boosters. Here was all-up testing at an even higher level than in Apollo, which had given the Saturn V two unmanned missions before committing a flight crew. The Roman poet Horace had written of men such as these:

> Oak and brass of triple fold
> Surrounded sure the heart that first made bold
> To the raging sea to trust a fragile bark.

But the flight lasted two days and generally went well. The cargo bay doors opened and then failed to close properly, but this caused no difficulty. The zero-gravity toilet broke down. A few tiles came off during re-entry, but the design allowed for this and their loss did not burn a hole in the spacecraft. In sum, the mission was a success. . . .

Plans for a Space Station

[Reagan] had high hopes for NASA; he saw the space program as an expression of his morning-in-America optimism. He also made a strong commitment on the military side [in] March [1983], by announcing the Strategic Defense Initiative with its goal of protecting the nation against Soviet missiles. Early in August, [White House aide Craig] Fuller arranged for him to host a luncheon for a group of business executives who hoped to pursue commercial activities in space. They told him that a space station would stimulate such activities, and Reagan replied, "I want a space station, too. I have wanted one for a long time." He made no commitment, but he came away fascinated and enthralled with what his guests had told him. . . .

As [Air Force Colonel Gilbert Rye] put it, "It was easy talking with Reagan about something he's enthused about, and he's enthused about space. He asked a lot of questions and wanted to know more about the various areas." [NASA administrator James] Beggs presented the space-station concept. [Budget director] David Stockman declared that the deficit would never go down if such projects were to go forward. William French Smith, the attorney general and another close friend of Reagan, responded: "I suspect the comptroller to King Ferdinand and Queen Isabella made the same pitch when Christopher Columbus came to court."

Reagan made no decision—not just then—but he met again with the principals a few days later. The question now involved a specific NASA request of $150 million with which to launch the space station as a project. This time Stockman conceded that NASA might indeed receive small budget increases during future years, and Reagan said, "Done!" He added, "I do not wish to be remembered only for El Salvador."

The president announced it openly in his State of the Union speech of January 1984. It is worth remembering this address, as a moment when hype could still substitute for actual accomplishment:

There is renewed energy and optimism throughout the land. America is back, standing tall.

A sparkling economy spurs initiative and ingenuity. Nowhere is this more true than our next frontier: space.

Nowhere do we so effectively demonstrate our technological leadership and ability to make life better on earth.

We can reach for greatness again. We can follow our dreams to distant stars, living and working in space for peaceful, economic, and scientific gain. Tonight, I am directing NASA to develop a permanently manned space station, and to do it within a decade.

A space station will permit quantum leaps in our research in science, communications, and in metals and lifesaving medicines which can be manufactured only in space.[1]

Putting All the Nation's Eggs in One Basket

NASA could share the sunshine of this hope, for the shuttle was now beginning to operate on a schedule, carrying out missions that pointed clearly toward the promise of the station. During 1984 and 1985, three missions focused on the repair and recovery of failed satellites. The first, the Solar Maximum Satellite, had reached orbit in 1980 to study the sun while it was very active, producing many sunspots and solar flares. *Challenger* rendezvoused with this craft; crew members replaced its attitude-control system and repaired a faulty instrument by installing new electronics. This work restored Solar Max to full operational status.

Subsequent flights succeeded with similar exercises. Early in 1984, *Challenger* had lifted two communication satellites. A malfunctioning rocket stage left them stranded uselessly in low orbit. In November a sister ship, *Discovery*, went up and recovered these valuable spacecraft, bringing them back to earth for eventual relaunch. . . .

In addition, NASA was approaching the day when the shuttle would monopolize U.S. launches. The agency was moving sharply away from expendable boosters, even though these rockets had been keeping up with the times. . . .

Yet the shuttle was proving to be a most fragile basket in which to place all the nation's eggs. The engines had been designed with the hope of making fifty-five flights before requiring major refurbishment. Instead, they had to be disassembled every three flights, to have their turbine blades replaced within the turbopumps. Each engine cost $36 million, and a combination of tight budgets and success-oriented management meant that there weren't many spares. As a result, minor problems with particular engines could disrupt the entire flight schedule.

In December 1981, a small accident at Rocketdyne tore loose an eight-inch pipe from the combustion chamber. Workers welded it back into place and tested the weld to be sure it would hold. It didn't. A year later, with this engine now mounted on the *Challenger* at Cape Canaveral, the weld cracked and leaked hydrogen during a test firing. This leak could have destroyed the shuttle by explosion; yet it took weeks to locate because it was in an inaccessible spot. NASA shipped a spare engine from Mississippi; it too had a welding crack. NASA shipped a second spare, and that did it, permitting a good flight. . . .

In addition, *Challenger* came close to disaster in August

Five members of the Challenger *crew: (front) Ronald E. McNair, Gregory E. Jarvis, Christa McAuliffe, (rear) Judith A. Resnick, and Ellison Onizuka.*

1983, because of a problem with one of its solid-rocket boosters. The lining of its exhaust nozzle eroded excessively during the rocket's two-minute burn. If it had fired for another eight seconds, the lining would have burned through. Six seconds later, the booster's hot flame would have breached the nozzle itself, as a prelude to a massive explosion.

The Pentagon had planned to become the shuttle's principal user, expecting to rely on it exclusively once it became fully operational. But in February 1984, Defense Secretary Weinberger approved a policy document stating that total reliance on the shuttle "represents an unacceptable national security risk." In June the Air Force gave NASA a sharp vote no confidence. It declared that it would remove ten payloads from the shuttle beginning in 1988 and fly them on expendables.

James Beggs was well aware that the Air Force might do this with many more payloads during subsequent years, and he was outraged. "The shuttle is the most reliable space transportation system ever built," he spluttered. The Air Force did not agree. It still would use the shuttle occasionally, but its prime launch vehicle would be another upgrade of Martin Marietta's Titan III. This firm now rebuilt it with new liquid-fueled engines that provided a 30 percent increase in thrust. They improved the performance so much that this new rocket gained the name Titan IV. It could lift up to 39,000 pounds to orbit. This made it very competitive with the shuttle, which had come in overweight and could only boost 47,000. To add insult to injury, the Titan IV could accommodate payloads that were physically larger than those the shuttle could carry. . . .

The Day of *Challenger*

Then came January 28, 1986: the day of *Challenger.*

The image remains seared in the nation's memory: the shuttle rising on its pillar of rocket exhaust, then an orange fireball, two solid boosters flying off crazily, and a shower of fragments that trailed smoke against the blue sky. One of those fragments was the cabin with its flight crew, who apparently remained conscious following the explosion. It took them more than two minutes to fall to the ocean from their initial altitude of nine miles. No parachutes were on board; when they struck the water, their deaths were swift.

The crew included a teacher, Christa McAuliffe, whom NASA had picked from among 11,400 applicants. This was part of a public-relations campaign to stir interest by demonstrating that the shuttle was safe enough for ordinary people. Senator Jake Garn, a strong supporter of NASA, had flown in this manner in April 1985. Congressman Bill Nelson had gone into orbit in similar fashion earlier in January.

The shuttle was indeed approaching routine operation, having made five flights in 1984 and nine in 1985. The latter year brought about a milestone: For the first time, the nation flew more shuttles than expendables. Fifteen flights were on the schedule for 1986, and NASA was pushing toward a goal of twenty-four by the end of the decade.

But the demand for an increasing flight rate put everyone under considerable pressure. Two important missions lay directly ahead. On May 15, *Challenger* was to launch Ulysses, a European probe that would swing around Jupiter and use its gravity to fly over the poles of the sun. Five days later, the Galileo spacecraft was to head for Jupiter itself. Both were to ride atop the Centaur upper stage, which would make its first flights within the shuttle. If either Ulysses or Galileo missed its launch date, it would have to wait thirteen months until the earth and Jupiter were once again in proper alignment.

The Cause of the Disaster

The cause of the disaster was in the solid-rocket boosters that flanked the main propellant tank. They were too large to fill with fuel or to transport in one piece; hence their builder, Morton Thiokol, had fabricated them in sections, to be assembled at the Cape. There was a gap between any two such segments, which had to be sealed to prevent hot gases at high pressure from leaking. The seal had two O-rings—thick rubber bands that encircled the twelve-foot diameter of the booster. When the booster's solid fuel ignited, a sudden pressure rise caused its casing to flex. The O-rings then needed enough resiliency to respond by flexing in concert, to maintain the seal's integrity. Each booster had three such sealed joints.

Prior to the disaster, O-rings had failed to hold on several earlier flights, because of erosion from the hot gases. A severe instance had occurred during a launch in April 1985, as rocket exhaust blew past the first O-ring and eroded up to 80 percent of the second one, within a limited area. The seal nevertheless held and the booster operated normally. But at Thiokol, engineers responsible for the seals became very concerned.

In July Roger Boisjoly, the company's senior seal specialist, wrote a memo to his vice president "to insure that management is fully aware of the seriousness of the current O-ring problem. It is my honest and very real fear that if we do not take immediate action to dedicate a team to solve the problem, we stand in jeopardy of losing a flight along with all the launch pad facilities."[2] Thiokol set up such a team, whose boss wrote a memo in October that began with the word "HELP!" and ended, "This is a red flag." However, there was no real urgency. Better seals were just one more improvement that would come along in good time, as the shuttle design continued to mature.

No clear criterion determined just when they might fail, but experience had shown that they worked best in warm weather, which made their rubber flexible and resilient. By contrast, chilly weather left them stiff, unable to flex quickly, and this was when they tended to show erosion and charring from the booster's flame. As the date for the *Challenger* flight approached, Florida was in the grip of an unusual cold wave. At Thiokol, Boisjoly and thirteen other engineers held a meeting and recommended unanimously that the launch be postponed.

This did not sit well with senior managers. They knew of the O-ring problem, but the experience of two dozen successful shuttle flights had bred complacency. The seals had worked before, however imperfectly; why not again? NASA had recently invited other firms to compete for Thiokol's solid-booster contract, placing the company under great pressure to show that it had a proper can-do spirit. Its vice president for space boosters, Joseph Kilminster, overruled Boisjoly's group and recommended launching *Challenger,* calling the available evidence "not conclusive."

NASA's Mistakes

Lawrence Mulloy, who managed Thiokol's contract at NASA's Marshall Space Flight Center, also wanted to press ahead. "My God, Thiokol, when do you want me to launch, next April?" he asked during the discussions. George Hardy, a deputy director at Marshall, added, "I'm appalled at your recommendations." Neither Hardy nor Mulloy would make the final decision, but they refrained from sharing the concerns of Thiokol's engineers with the Cape Canaveral officials who had the authority to delay the launch. Still, despite the opposition from NASA-Marshall, Thiokol's engineering managers held their ground. Presented with a formal statement approving the launch, Allan McDonald, the company's senior man at the Cape, refused to sign.

Three-foot icicles were forming on the launch tower during the launch preparations, hanging downward like daggers. But late that morning the sun came out and melted the ice, relieving last-minute concerns. As the engines fired and the shuttle started to lift, a puff of black smoke appeared alongside the bottom joint in one of the solid boosters. The seal had momentarily failed to flex. It quickly did so, and no more smoke appeared, but the harm had been done. This seal now was a damaged gasket that soon would blow.

It gave way completely in a small area some fifty-nine seconds into the flight, as a small flame appeared along the side of this rocket. The flame quickly spread and burned like a blowtorch, both at the propellant tank and at a strut that secured this booster. Within seconds, the liquid hydrogen began to ignite. The tank ruptured; the solid booster broke free of its strut and slammed into it, breaking it open like an egg full of explosives. The tank and the shuttle orbiter disintegrated. "I do not know how many seconds it took for the sound of the blast to travel down," wrote a reporter from the Los Angeles *Times*. "When it arrived, it did so like a thunderclap, rattling the metal grandstands. And then it abruptly ceased, replaced by a strange and terrible quiet."

This stillness at Canaveral led to the swift appointment of a presidential commission, which found flaws not only in O-rings but in NASA itself. The commission's chairman was William Rogers, a former secretary of state. Noting that Thiokol had faced the possible loss of its contract, he told Mulloy that its officials "were under a lot of pressure to give you the answer you wanted. And they construed what you and Mr. Hardy said to mean that you wanted them to change their minds."

John Young, the chief of NASA's astronauts, wrote bitterly of the seals, noting: "There is only one driving reason that such a potentially dangerous system would ever be allowed to fly—schedule pressure." The commission's report stated that as problems with the seals "grew in number and severity, NASA minimized them in briefings and reports; as tests and then flights confirmed damage to the sealing rings, the reaction by both NASA and Thiokol was to increase the amount of damage considered 'acceptable.'" Richard Feynman, a Nobel Prize–winning physicist from Caltech who was known for speaking his mind, warned that "NASA exaggerates the reliability of its product to the point of fantasy." He then pronounced the *Challenger*'s epitaph: "For a successful technology, reality must take precedence over public relations, for Nature cannot be fooled."[3]

Three orbiters remained: *Discovery, Columbia,* and *Atlantis,* which had joined the fleet in 1985. In addition, Gil Rye had arranged for Rockwell International to build major portions of a new orbiter. It later took shape as a replacement named *Endeavour*. But in other respects, NASA and the Air Force took several large steps away from the shuttle. It still would play its role, but the goal now was a mixed fleet, in which expendable launch vehicles would receive due attention.

A Severe Setback for the Space Program

In NASA's hour of crisis, Reagan turned to [former NASA administrator] James Fletcher, prevailing upon him to return to this agency as its head. In June, NASA scrubbed plans to use Centaur as a shuttle upper stage, leaving Galileo and Ulysses in the lurch. This decision reflected new concern for danger; Centaur burned liquid hydrogen and oxygen, and there was no way to abort a shuttle flight and vent the propellants for a safe landing. Late that summer, NASA also canceled most of its planned Spacelab flights. It had flown four to date; the next one would not fly until December 1990.

The Air Force did more, and it had the clout to do it. Prior to the Reagan administration, the Pentagon's space budget had been only half the size of NASA's. In 1986, with the Strategic Defense Initiative setting the pace amid a host of highly classified new programs, this budget reached $17 billion, more than twice that of NASA.

The Air Force had built a launch complex for the shuttle at Vandenberg that cost $3 billion. It now went into mothballs. Air Force Secretary Edward Aldridge expanded the earlier purchase of ten heavy-lift Titan IV launchers, ordering another thirteen. He also had nearly seventy Titan II ICBMs, most of them deployed operationally in their silos; he now stepped up efforts to refurbish thirteen of them, for use as launch vehicles. He was well aware that both versions could fly with the Centaur, whereas the shuttle couldn't.

Still, for the moment the nation's space program rested on its limited stockpile of Titans, Atlases, and Deltas that were left over from earlier purchases. The Air Force had seven Titan IIIs, and on April 18, one of them lifted off from Vandenberg, carrying a Hexagon reconnaissance satellite. This mission was important; another Titan III had splashed into the Pacific the previous August. This one did not even get that far. Eight seconds after liftoff, one of its solid boosters blew up, touching off an explosion of the entire vehicle. A blazing pyrotechnic shower caused damage to the launch pad that took seven months to repair, while the Titan III went in for the same scrutiny as the shuttle. It did not fly again for a year and a half.

On May 3 it was the turn of NASA, as it launched a GOES weather satellite aboard a Delta. This rocket was known for its reliability, having flown successfully on its previous forty-three launches, but this time its number came up. Its engine shut down some seventy seconds into the flight. This was serious, though less so than in the case of the *Challenger;* a military Delta would fly again, with success, as early as September. But NASA had exactly two Deltas left in its inventory.

Just then, in the spring of 1986, the only NASA boosters certified for flight were three Atlas-Centaurs, all committed in advance to specific payloads The Air Force had its own supply of Atlases, but these lacked significant upper stages and could only lift spacecraft of modest size. During 1986, NASA and the Air Force together carried out only four successful launches via Titan, Atlas, and Delta, though twenty would have been more like it if they could have used the shuttle. This was the smallest number since 1959. It rose to seven in 1987 and fell back to six in 1988; not until 1989 would the national space program begin to recover. "We have an unqualified disaster on our hands," said Albert Wheelon [head of the CIA's satellite program] shortly after the Titan III explosion of April 1986. "We are essentially out of business."

1. *New York Times*, Jan. 26, 1984, p. B8.

2. Boisjoly. Quoted in *Scientific American*, Aug. 1986, pp. 62–63.

3. *Science*, Mar. 14, 1986, p. 1238; Mar. 28, 1986, p. 1495; June 20, 1986, p. 1488; Feynman, *What Do You Care*, pp. 223, 237; Los Angeles *Times*, Jan. 28, 1996, p. A3.

The *Exxon Valdez* Oil Spill

Brad Knickerbocker

On the morning of March 24, 1989, the oil tanker *Exxon Valdez* ran aground in Alaska's Prince William Sound, resulting in the worst environmental disaster in U.S. history. Over 10 million barrels of oil spilled into the sound, killing wildlife and crippling the local salmon and fishing industries. The spill was initially blamed on the tanker's captain, Joseph Hazelwood, who had reportedly been drinking that night. Later it was revealed that Exxon had cut back on the number of crewmen running the ship in order to save money; several lawsuits against Exxon followed. In addition to the placing of blame, a massive cleanup operation ensued, along with efforts to prevent future oil spills. In the following article, Brad Knickerbocker, a staff reporter for the *Christian Science Monitor*, describes the legacy of the *Exxon Valdez* ten years after the spill.

I t was just past midnight on a Good Friday, a clear, calm night in Alaska's Prince William Sound, when the tanker captain's voice crackled over the radio.

"We've fetched up—ah—hard aground north of Goose Island off Bligh Reef, and—ah—evidently leaking some oil," Joseph Hazelwood told the Coast Guard Marine Safety Office back in Valdez, a somber resignation in his tone. "We're gonna be here for a while."

Excerpted from "The Big Spill," by Brad Knickerbocker, *The Christian Science Monitor*, March 22, 1999. Copyright ©1999 by The Christian Science Publishing Society. Reprinted with permission from *The Christian Science Monitor*.

"Some oil" turned out to be an estimated 11 million gallons of North Slope crude bound for Los Angeles and now oozing out of the ruptured 987-foot *Exxon Valdez* in what would become the United States' worst environmental disaster.

The sight of cleanup workers futilely trying to hose off oiled rocks and gathering the carcasses of dead seals and birds shocked a world hungry for the oil that heats its homes and powers its vehicles.

But that 1989 event also has spurred new laws and procedures designed to prevent future spills and to respond more quickly and effectively if one should occur. It's also provided scientists with an unprecedented laboratory for studying the effects of marine pollution.

Motoring over the sound on a sparkling late-winter day with bush pilot Patrick Kearney, snow-capped Chugach Mountains plummeting to dark blue waters as a stunning backdrop, the sound today looks as healthy as ever. But some *Exxon Valdez* oil from 10 years ago still can be found here, lodged under rocks on places like Knight Island.

"You can actually see a sheen coming off the beaches on a hot summer day," says Mark King, a fisherman from Cordova who's had his own boat since he was 13.

Campers and kayakers still avoid parts of the shoreline. And according to government scientists, the oil continues to hamper the recovery of what once was pristine habitat for countless seals, shore birds, killer whales, salmon, and other species.

"The ecosystem is well on its way to recovery, but the long-term impacts on individual populations may take decades to fully heal," says Molly McCammon, executive director of the Exxon Valdez Oil Spill Trustee Council, a coalition of federal and state agencies set up in 1991 to oversee restoration efforts.

In fact, according to the council's latest findings, only two of 23 injured species—bald eagles and river otters—have fully recovered. Pink salmon, Pacific herring, sea otters, and mussels are making a comeback. But harbor seals, killer whales, and harlequin ducks "are showing little or no clear improvement since spill injuries occurred," says the council.

Warring Viewpoints

But Exxon—which hired its own scientists—maintains that "the environment in Prince William Sound is healthy, robust, and thriving."

"Certainly there were severe short-term impacts on many species due to the spilled oil, and they suffered damages," acknowledges the Texas-based oil company, which paid nearly $3 billion in cleanup and compensation costs (but is appealing a $5 billion punitive award to fishermen, native Americans, and Alaskan communities). "But there has been no long-term damage caused by the spilled oil."

No one disputes the spill's death toll during the spring and summer of 1989 as thick oil spread over 10,000 square miles, contaminating a national forest, four national wildlife refuges, three national parks, five state parks, four "critical habitat areas," and a state game sanctuary along 1,500 miles of Alaska shoreline. Casualties included 2,800 sea otters, 300 harbor seals, 250 bald eagles, as many as 22 killer whales, and an estimated quarter-million seabirds. It's unclear how many billions of salmon and herring eggs and intertidal plants succumbed to oil smothering.

One reason is that no one knows exactly how much oil leaked for the 10 hours before help arrived and days afterward. The Coast Guard says "more than 11 million gallons." Some who helped clean it up say more than 30 million gallons of the 53 million gallons on board could have been lost. The difference is important, because penalties against Exxon were based on the size of the spill, as were new regulations for spill prevention.

In any case, scientists at the National Oceanic and Atmospheric Administration's Auk Bay fisheries laboratory in Juneau found oil to be "much more toxic and persistent in the environment than previously thought."

"The results from the long-term studies following the spill have surprised us," these scientists reported recently.

"Oil is 100 times more toxic to developing fish than previously thought," meaning that very small amounts—parts per billion, or the equivalent of a teaspoon in an Olympic-sized swimming pool—are believed to cause genetic damage resulting in "higher mortality rates in eggs, more deformed juveniles, and less growth and survival in adults."

"This spill has basically changed the way we understand the effects of oil in a marine ecosystem," says Riki Ott, a marine biologist whose doctoral studies at the University of Washington in Seattle focused on ocean pollution. "We understand now that oil is toxic at way lower levels, and it causes multigenerational effects."

Government scientists think this is why wild salmon and

 ## The Symbolic Value of the *Exxon Valdez* Oil Spill

The symbolic and emotional power of oil spills is undeniable. Spills have been labeled "one of the most highly visible and emotion-causing forms of ocean pollution." The primary images of oil spills in the 1960s, 1970s, and 1980s include black, gooey oil washing ashore, oiled wildlife, and workers struggling to clean up the small fraction of oil that can actually be recovered from a spill. . . .

The dominant symbols of the *Exxon Valdez* spill were those of oiled otters and birds, the soiling of the seemingly pristine Alaskan environment, and the image of a large, uncaring oil company that employed a drunk tanker captain, spilled oil, and then failed to manage the cleanup. [As one reporter explains,] "Television images of dead otters and oily birds instantly became archetypes of corporate rapacity and incompetence, and associated Exxon permanently in the public mind with blackened beaches and drunken sea captains." The accuracy of these images is far less important than their symbolic and emotive effects; the images convey the notion that something is wrong and that something must be done. . . .

herring runs remain below historic levels. Both fish are commercially valuable, and their initial "crash" and incomplete recovery have meant continuing bad news for thousands of fishermen.

But beyond the impact on human livelihoods, the herring situation has been felt across the ecosystem. Herring are high-calorie, high-fat fish preferred by harbor seals and many seabirds—animals farther up the food chain who have yet to fully recover.

Studies also show that some intertidal mussel beds here still are contaminated. Mussels can withstand the pollution, but the animals that feed on them—such as juvenile sea otters and harlequin ducks—continue to have elevated

---

In the Exxon Valdez accident, the special symbolic value of Alaska compounded Exxon's problems, particularly when set against the negative symbol of Big Oil. Alaska invokes images of a wild, isolated, and beautiful place—The Last Frontier—unspoiled by humans. This imagery has been promoted in journalism and the arts for years, from Jack London's and Robert Service's stories and poems about the North to writings about Alaska by John Muir, John McPhee, and James Michener. The oil industry itself long promoted this rugged image as part of its advertising. The industry could therefore promote its technical prowess in extracting oil in a remote and harsh environment while greatly minimizing the environmental effects of that extraction.

The spill thus reopened a dormant oil-versus-environment debate at the national level, not just within the confines of Alaskan politics. Oil interests in Alaska and elsewhere found their ability to influence the terms of the debate overwhelmed by the sheer size of the spill, by national news exposure, and by the juxtaposition of Alaska as beautiful and pristine with images of the oil industry as dirty, uncaring, and dangerous.

Thomas A. Birkland, "In the Wake of the *Exxon Valdez:* How Environmental Disasters Influence Policy," *Environment*, Spring 1998.

levels of mortality in places hardest hit by the spill.

Part of the argument over the degree of recovery stems from a lack of pre-spill baseline scientific knowledge of Prince William Sound. Among other things, the area has seen a slight rise in average temperatures in recent years that may be having an effect on wildlife here beyond that caused by oil pollution.

Ocean as a Petri Dish

Jane Lubchenco, a marine biologist at Oregon State University in Corvallis, says, "It really is a myth that the oceans are so vast that we can't affect them."

"The reality is that we are changing the chemistry of the oceans, we're changing the physical structure, and we're changing the biology of oceans—especially coastal systems," says Dr. Lubchenco. "And the sum total of those changes has not really been appreciated by most folks."

Here in Prince William Sound, those changes are very much appreciated as the restoration work continues.

And whatever became of the *Exxon Valdez*? Ten years later, the infamous ship has been renamed the *SeaRiver Mediterranean*, banished from Alaskan waters, and now carries Mideast oil to European ports.

Ex-captain Hazelwood, now working as a claims adjuster in a New York law office, soon will begin 1,000 hours of community service picking up trash along Alaskan highways. He was cleared of a charge of piloting the tanker while drunk, but was convicted of negligently discharging oil. A great deal of oil.

CHAPTER 4

Culture and Entertainment

Pop Culture in the '80s: Plenty of Pleasant Distractions

Myron A. Marty

In his book, *Daily Life in the United States, 1960–1990: Decades of Discord,* Myron A. Marty describes the effects that major events, such as the Cold War, the social revolutions of the 1960s, the Vietnam War, and Watergate, had on American culture. He characterizes the 1980s as a time when Americans sought to escape from issues such as economic stability or national security. In the excerpt that follows, Marty, a professor of history at Drake University, describes some of the most popular cultural trends of the period.

Although Americans in the 1980s enjoyed a cafeteria of entertainment possibilities, the main fare for most remained television. Thanks to the Federal Communications Commission (FCC), what they watched on TV underwent certain changes. Mark Fowler, appointed by President Reagan to head the FCC, regarded television as just another appliance, "a toaster with pictures," that should be treated like a business, nothing more or less. Under Fowler's leadership, the FCC in 1981 discontinued rules limiting the number of minutes per hour that could be devoted to advertising and stopped requiring television stations to play a public service role.

A 1990 Gallup poll showed that the percentage of persons who considered watching television as their favorite way to spend an evening declined from 46 percent in 1974 to 24 percent in 1990, no doubt reflecting their complaints about the quality of programming. During these years, dining out, going to movies or the theater, playing cards and other games, dancing, and listening to music showed comparably sharp declines in popularity. Taking their places were activities not included in the 1974 survey, such as jogging, working in crafts, and gardening. Reading and spending time at home with the family showed slight increases. Nonetheless, the average American spent some twenty-eight hours in front of a television set each week. Many of those were daytime hours, as soap operas and talk shows remained popular. . . .

Television Diversifies

Cable Television. The continued diversification and extension of programming through cable channels meant that television did even less to pull families together than it had done in the past. Sometimes it had the opposite effect. For example, when MTV, a thoroughly postmodern cable channel, was launched in 1981 and aimed particularly at teenagers by bringing twenty-four hours of rock videos and commercials daily into millions of homes, adults expected their children to watch it in their own rooms with doors closed. Within two years of its arrival, MTV claimed to have viewers in 14 million homes daily.

As MTV evolved, it brought greater variety and creativity to its programming, responding to initial criticisms that it favored established groups of white artists and presented objectionable anti-female images. Being featured on MTV boosted sales of the performers' records by some 15 to 20 percent. MTV appearances also made stars, among the most notable being Michael Jackson and Madonna. Experimentation by MTV with postmodern cultural styles paved the way for comparable experiments in programs like *Miami Vice.* . . .

By the end of the 1980s, with service reaching into

nearly 60 percent of American homes, cable television seemed to be approaching a saturation point. Households without it probably could not afford it or simply did not want it. Nonetheless, its existence in more than 50 million households meant a further diffusion of viewing audiences and a decline in the influence of the old, established networks. Indeed, by 1990 ABC, CBS, and NBC claimed less than 60 percent of viewing time. Remote control units no doubt weakened the grip of the major networks and fragmented viewing audiences further. Before it became standard equipment in most homes, TV watchers tuned in to a single channel and stayed with it for a whole show, enduring or ignoring commercials. Remote control changed all that, as viewers hit 'mute" buttons during commercials or "grazed" up and down the spectrum of channels to see what else was playing. Viewers' starting point might have been a network station, but their landing place may have been a cable channel. . . .

Network Programs. Two of the most popular new network shows of the early 1980s *The Cosby Show* and *Family Ties,* reworked the themes of 1950s sitcoms, the former featuring a middle-class black family. Before the end of the decade *Roseanne,* starring Roseanne Barr as a factory worker and joke-telling wife and mother, replaced *The Cosby Show* at the top of the sitcom ratings. Some regarded these programs as a contest between blue-collar chic and black-family chic. Also popular at the decade's end was a prime-time animated cartoon, *The Simpsons.* The fact that this satiric family comedy ran on the new Fox network and challenged *The Cosby Show* in head-to-head competition was another indication of the loss of dominance by the big-three networks, ABC, CBS, and NBC. . . .

VCRs. As alternatives to commercial and public television, viewers increasingly turned to rental of videotapes. By the end of the 1980s homes equipped with videocassette players rented, on average, two to three videos each month. In homes that included persons ages 18 to 29 the rentals were more numerous, and they were much lower in those with persons age 60 and older. Rental of videos represented a $13 billion market. In 1987, the film industry's revenue from rentals, along with that from films shown on cable television, surpassed its income from ticket sales. Many owners, surveys showed, never learned how to program their VCRs for taping shows to be replayed later and used them only for rented tapes. As VCRs grew in popularity, so did camcorders for recording instant versions of home movies—especially in 1990 when they became much smaller and offered longer playback times.

Print Media Endures

Newspapers. Newspapers had difficulty competing with television for readers' time. . . .

Perhaps the biggest change in the newspaper business occurred in 1982 when the Gannett Company, owner of a chain of dailies, launched *USA Today.* This national newspaper made explicit attempts to compete with television as a primary source of news. Boxes dispensing it on street comers displayed the front page in windows that looked like television screens. News reports and features were brief and crisply written, and pictures, often in color, were more plentiful than in other newspapers. The fast-glimpse qualities of *USA Today* inspired critics to compare its fare with that offered in fast-food restaurants. McNews, they called it. Within the next several years Gannett also acquired a number of major newspapers, including the *Detroit News,* the *Des Moines Register,* and the *Louisville Courier-Journal* and *Louisville Times.* Although Gannett-owned newspapers maintained individual identities, they also reflected traits displayed most prominently by *USA Today,* such as the shortened news reports, and readers detected a loss of local flavor in the papers' coverage.

Following *USA Today*'s lead, other newspapers printed more pictures in color and abbreviated their reporting. Perhaps this enabled them to remain a staple in the life of the two-thirds of American adults who read them daily. Only one in five of the readers spent more than 30 minutes with the daily paper, and they tended to be older and better-educated. Meanwhile television continued to grow as the main source of news for the American people, partly because the network anchors seemed like authoritative guests in many homes, and partly because of the news coverage of CNN.

Magazines. Big-circulation magazines intended for general audiences saw their sales slump as their traditional readership was aging and dying. Smaller, more precisely targeted magazines fared better, as did some fashion magazines. The wide range of choices, symbolic of postmodern conditions, no doubt encouraged browsing rather than selecting one magazine and staying with it. Reflecting the get-rich climate of the times, *Forbes,* one of the nation's leading business magazines, saw its circulation grow and the median age of its readers move downward.

Books. By the end of the 1980s total book sales approached $15 billion, double the amount recorded at the beginning of the decade. Much of publishers' revenue came from the works of bestselling authors. Stephen King landed ten horror novels on bestseller lists during the decade, and Danielle Steele eight romances. Sometimes outstanding works like Umberto Eco's *The Name of the Rose* and Toni Morrison's *Beloved* also became bestsellers, promising to become classics. . . .

Oscar Winners and Blockbusters

Movies. The diverse tastes of producers and audiences were evident in the variety of films winning honors each year. In 1982, for example, *Gandhi,* the story of the man who led India's struggle for independence, won an Oscar for Best Picture. Several years later the Oscar went to *Amadeus,* which treated the life of the great composer Wolfgang Amadeus Mozart. Then came *Out of Africa* and *The Last Emperor,* the latter being the story of a bygone China. Named Best Picture in 1988 was *Rain Man,* starring Dustin Hoffman who was named Best Actor for his performance; this film introduced audiences to autism, a baffling mental disorder. It was followed by *Driving Miss Daisy,* with Jessica Tandy playing the role of an eccentric but lovable elderly woman and winning Best Actress for it. Then came *Dances with Wolves* directed by and featuring Kevin Costner (Best Director) in a romanticized story of the Lakota Sioux nation.

Award-winning films were often bested at the box office by those featuring daring themes or techniques. That explains the success of the 1981 blockbuster *Raiders of the Lost Ark,* and another in 1982, *E.T.—The Extra-Terrestrial,* the story of love between an Earth boy, lonely in suburbia, and a stranded alien from space. Both were directed by Steven Spielberg. *E.T.* grossed $228 million at the box office and demonstrated the commercial success that lay in embedding a film's vocabulary ("Elliot," "Ouch," and "Phone Home") into the language of everyday life and in marketing a film's images on such things as lunch boxes, bicycles, and even underwear. Another blockbuster success was Tim Burton's *Batman* in 1989. Although it did not match the revenue produced by *E.T.*, the "Batmania" it inspired paid dividends to marketers of products bearing the image or logo of the Batman.

Sylvester Stallone's *Rambo: First Blood, Part II* is a good example of a popular film featuring violence. Stallone played the role of a Vietnam veteran who freed prisoners of war, thereby exposing the alleged indifference of the U.S. government. The film's pro-war perspective drew complaints by those who thought it tried to revise truths about the war, but the complaints did not keep Rambo from becoming a folk hero or Rambo guns and knives from becoming popular children's toys.

Movie Ratings. In 1984 the Motion Picture Association of America (MPAA) added a new rating, PG-13, the first change since the introduction of the rating system sixteen years earlier. The new rating placed films between PG (parental guidance suggested) and R (restricted). It was "advisory" in that it did not exclude viewers under age 14, but it informed parents that violence or other content in the film might not be suitable for their children. In 1990 the

MPAA replaced the controversial X rating, which had come to be regarded as synonymous with pornography, with NC-17. The new rating was intended for movies that despite depictions of explicit sex or extreme violence, such as *Henry & June,* were regarded as serious artistic efforts.

Concerns over Popular Music

Radio. As it had done with television, the Federal Communications Commission in 1981 discontinued rules limiting the number of minutes per hour devoted to advertising on radio and requiring stations to commit 6 to 8 percent of their programming time to news and public affairs. The FCC also attempted to deal with "shock radio" by ruling that stations were free to air "indecent material" between midnight and 6 A.M., when children would be least likely to hear it. This 1987 action did not define indecent, however, and broadcasters felt free to fill their programs with whatever listeners were willing to tolerate. To the satisfaction of broadcasters, the FCC in the same year abolished what was called the fairness doctrine, which required radio and television stations to broadcast all sides of controversial issues. . . .

Popular Music. By the 1980s, the rock music young people had found so appealing and their elders so appalling in earlier decades enjoyed a large measure of acceptance in mainstream America. Indeed, it became a standard feature of mainstream advertising. One reason is that the teenagers of the 1960s did not forsake their earlier tastes in music when they reached their thirties. Another reason is that rock music lost much of its shock quality. A third is that the varieties of rock music were so plentiful that persons who did not like one variety had plenty of other choices. The same was true of performing groups. Fans could love one and detest another. Consequently, variations of rock music thrived alongside of country music, surf music, jazz, disco, and a new arrival, Jamaican reggae. . . .

Worries about Popular Music. Rock music's lyrics, with themes of sex and violence, worried many. The National

PTA and the Parents' Music Resource Center (a group based in Washington, D.C.) urged the Recording Industry Association of America to rate its records in a system similar to the one used for motion pictures. The Association refused to do so, but it recommended that its members label some of their records "Explicit Lyrics—Parental Advisory." Such measures did not appease rock music's harshest critics. Allan Bloom, a professor at the University of Chicago, seemed to reflect their sentiments in his attack on rock music in his bestselling *The Closing of the American Mind*. He contended that rock music "has one appeal only, a barbaric appeal, to sexual desire—not love, not *eros,* but sexual desire undeveloped and untutored. . . . Rock gives children, on a silver platter, with all the public authority of the entertainment industry, everything parents always used to tell them they had to wait for until they grew up and would understand later."[1]

Rap Music. Those who worried about rock music had more to worry about when rap became popular in the late 1980s. . . .

Before the end of the decade the lyrics of several rap groups, such as Slick Rick and 2 Live Crew, drew sharp criticism for their explicit description of sexual organs and activities and for seeming to encourage violence against women. To many, the lyrics were offensive or unintelligible. When a sheriff in Florida brought an obscenity complaint against a store owner for selling records of 2 Live Crew, a U.S. District judge convicted the owner after months of hearings. The leader of 2 Live Crew and two band members were arrested and brought to trial, too, but a jury found them not guilty of obscenity charges. The jury foreman acknowledged that members of the jury found it difficult to understand the key piece of evidence, a tape recording of the performance that had led to the defendants' arrest.

Classical Music. The difficulties faced by symphony orchestras, opera companies, and composers suggested that classical music was no longer a central feature of American culture. Operating deficits were common. Listening audiences had never been diverse, but in the words of an anonymous administrator quoted by the *New York Times,* they were now "white, rich, and almost dead." Portions of their audiences were tired of the standby classical pieces by great composers of the past; other portions had no use for the avant-garde works of contemporary composers. Imitations of classical forms by contemporary composers did not work either.

Moreover, as younger generations matured they generally failed to replace their popular tastes, which were so different from those of previous generations of youth, with classical ones. Linda Sanders explained it this way in *Civilization*: "It was one thing for educated adults to tell hormone-crazed teenagers back in the 1950s that 'Blue Suede Shoes' was worthless trash. It was quite another for educated adults to try to tell other educated adults in the 1980s that blues, reggae, and minimalism (or, for that matter, the Beatles, Bruce Springsteen and Prince) were either musically or spiritually inferior to Bach and Beethoven."[2] Add to this the sense maturing generations' opinion that classical music was for the intellectual and social elite, and it is easy to see why classical music was losing its appeal and its audiences. . . .

Board and Video Games

Games. Board games have long been a popular diversion for children. Monopoly, for example, a Parker Brothers game, has been around since 1935. To celebrate its golden anniversary in 1985, it held championship matches in Atlantic City, New Jersey, with the winner receiving $15,140—the equivalent of the total play money in the Monopoly game. Scrabble, a word game invented by James Brunot in 1948, remained popular. Game players were ready for something new, however, when Trivial Pursuit arrived from Canada in 1983. Sales figures are a good way of measuring the impact of a new arrival. At one point there were back orders for a million games, and in its first year sales of Trivial Pursuit totaled $777 million. (What kind of questions did Trivial Pursuit ask? Ones like this: "Who invented Trivial Pursuit?") In Pictionary, another board game, players advanced by deciphering their teammates' pencil drawings. Introduced in Seattle in 1985, its sales reached $3 million in 1987 and continued upward.

Sales of board games were no match for the electronic games that became increasingly popular after the introduction of Atari in the mid-1970s and Pac-Man in 1981. The first ones were played as attachments to television sets, but before long they were separate gadgets in a variety of shapes and sizes. When Nintendo came along in 1985 it started running up big numbers: Sales amounted to $830 million in 1987 and exceeded $3 billion in 1990. Electronic toys, unlike board games, could be played alone and therefore required no communication and interaction among children. . . .

A Fitness Craze Sweeps America
Even as Pro Sports Face Problems

Sports. Major-league baseball tested its place in the hearts of many Americans when a seven-week players' strike interrupted the 1981 season. The strike caused the middle third of the schedule to be canceled, resulting in the major leagues' first split season. The origins of the discord between players and management lay in legal actions taken by players in the mid-seventies to gain the right for veteran players to sign with other teams as free agents. When the owners' absolute power over players was broken, they established a system that required the loss of a free agent to be compensated in the form of a player from the team with which the free agent had signed. In the impasse that followed, fans were caught in the middle and left with a gameless midsummer.

In 1982 the National Football League (NFL) faced a similar situation. No games were played during a 57-day strike. In 1987, though, when the season was interrupted by a 24-day strike by players over rules surrounding the free agency of players, management canceled games on the first weekend but then fielded teams made up of replacement players and regulars who drifted back. When the players decided to go back to work, the owners told them they could not play immediately and would not be paid. The National Labor Relations Board ruled in the players' favor and ordered the NFL to pay striking players more than $20 million in lost wages and incentive bonuses for the game they had missed. As with baseball, the fans were on the sidelines—mostly disgusted with both players and management.

Olympics. The United States hosted the 1984 Summer Olympics in Los Angeles. Broadcast by ABC, the event's 168 hours on the air drew ratings higher than expected, and it produced several heroes: Carl Lewis won gold medals in the 100-meter dash, the 200-meter dash, the 400-meter relay, and the long jump, duplicating what Jesse Owens had done in 1936 in Berlin. In contrast to earlier times, the rules of the Olympics allowed Lewis to earn about $1 million yearly and still compete as an amateur. Another hero was the Olympics' real crowd pleaser, Mary Lou Retton, a 16-year-old whose five medals included a gold in all-around gymnastics. Her feat gained her many commercial endorsements.

By 1988 the Olympics were greeted as welcome television fare by millions of viewers. To accommodate their interests, the Winter Games, held in Calgary, Canada, were extended to sixteen days. . . .

Fitness. Physical fitness participants in this decade wanted to look good, feel good, lose weight, have fun, make friends, develop personal discipline, and, above all, stay well. Avid runners claimed that running gave them more daily energy, sharpened their mental edge, kept them in good physical condition, and increased their resistance to illness. Tennis players were just as avid about their sport, although they made fewer claims for its benefits. Bowlers, golfers, skiers, bikers, and participants in other sports were avid, too, but their fitness claims were less audible. Many of them considered their participation as recreational rather than fitness-driven.

Private health clubs eagerly exploited the fitness interests of many Americans. The number of clubs increased from 7,500 in 1980 (not including YMCAs or golf, tennis, and other sports-specific clubs) to more than 20,000 by the end of the decade. Membership in health and fitness clubs reached about 40 million before the end of the decade. The quest for fitness could be satisfied in one's home, too, as the popularity of *Jane Fonda's Workout Book* (1981) bears witness. In addition to providing an exercise regimen, this book by an actress-turned-political-activist and now fitness promoter included dietary advice and musings on ways for women to maintain good health. A bestseller, it opened the way to Fonda's further commercial ventures—exercise studios, cassette tapes with music to accompany workouts, and an exercise video. Other exercise promoters, such as Richard Simmons, also produced videos for use at home, and sales of home exercise equipment by Nordic Track, Nautilus, and other companies boomed. So did sales of improved equipment for outdoor sports.

1. Allan Bloom, *The Closing of the American Mind* (New York: Simon & Schuster, 1987), 73, 80–81.

2. Linda Sanders, "Facing the Music," *Civilization*, May/June 1996, 38–39.

The Revolution Will Be Televised: Pop Music of the '80s

Paul Friedlander

Paul Friedlander is assistant dean at the Conservatory of Music at the University of the Pacific. In the following selection, he examines the major trends in popular music in the 1980s, especially the creation of MTV and its effect on the music industry. He also discusses Bruce Springsteen's political, working-class rock; Michael Jackson's sudden rise to megastardom; and Madonna's emergence as a symbol of sexual power. Finally, Friedlander examines controversial heavy metal music, as well as the growth of rap music and its influence on American culture.

The Rock/Pop landscape in the eighties was filled with a number of different styles that were arranged and formatting neatly on radio dials across the country. Rock dinosaurs like the Rolling Stones, Led Zeppelin, Paul McCartney, the Doobie Brothers, and Rod Stewart were still significant players on album-oriented rock (AOR) radio, the dominant rock format for youthful American listeners. In addition to Led Zeppelin, AOR also sported middle-of-the-road hard rockers like Foreigner, Journey, Styx, Rush, and Bob Seeger and his Silver Bullet Band. Pop-rockers like Neil Diamond, Linda Ronstadt, Diana Ross, and Olivia Newton-John populated the softer adult contemporary

(A/C) stations that appealed more to women and an older pop-rock clientele.

Punk-influenced new music (the so-called "new wave") was just budding on radio, however; within a few years it would proliferate and cover the media. The key ingredient in new wave's success was the linkage of music and video, a dynamic that was institutionalized with the birth of MTV (Music Television) on August 1, 1981. At a time of Reagan administration deregulation and declining record sales, the Warner Bros. conglomerate, in partnership with American Express, took a chance. They created a twenty-four-hour television channel, beaming to a target audience of twelve- to thirty-four-year-olds music videos much the same way that radio broadcast songs. . . .

Music Videos: From Artistic Expression to Commercialism

In MTV's early years it was the more eclectic artists who were most likely to produce videos. Thus, MTV introduced numerous new wave selections to its viewing public. However, radio viewed MTV as a threat and did its best to denigrate the new format. Yet when Men at Work scored two #1 singles without significant radio airplay, MTV pointed out that the band's videos were in heavy rotation on the channel. Exposure on MTV sold records, influenced buying habits, and provided exposure for unknown artists. Beginning in 1984 MTV charged record companies for broadcasting videos (until that time it had been free).

What may have initially been the impulse by musicians to expand artistic expression to the visual dimension was, by middecade, recognized as an important way for record companies to promote product. Major labels viewed music videos essentially as TV commercials, designed to sell merchandise. Writer Simon Frith points out that in using videos the labels were also trying to help create, by emphasizing a particular visual image or identity, new audiences for their artists. Also by middecade numerous media analysts were exploring the impact of the new marriage between rock music and video. Music videos capitalized on what Frith asserts were contemporary rock music values of brash individualism, impatience, youthful rebellion, and sensual delight. Lynch identified effective cinematic techniques such as dissolves, split screens, superimpositions, backlighting, and intercutting among others. In other words, music video equals "Miami Vice" equals movies.

Many critics felt that music videos reinforced negative trends already occurring in society. Kids already sat passively in front of a box, waiting for the "answer." This supported President Reagan's penchant for simplistic explanations and solutions for society's growing problems. Some also felt that when song became video, the consequence was to lose the music; story, image, and style took precedence. In addition, others cited the issues of authenticity and lip synching. The practice of lip synching (pantomiming words to hit songs) was the practice on Dick Clark's "American Bandstand" for decades. Music videos required artists to lip synch their songs. For some, this practice merely confirmed John Lennon's pronouncement in "Strawberry Fields" that "nothing is real." The Milli Vanilli scandal didn't help matters. (It was revealed that this male duo not only didn't sing on their record, but used a tape of their voices during five concerts.) Though it was not uncommon in the eighties for performers to "double" their voices electronically in concert (or, as in the case of the vocal group the Nylons, use additional voices on tape), lip synching a "live" show stretched artistic credibility.

In its early years MTV had a democratizing or pluralistic impact on the music industry. It introduced new and less mainstream artists to mainstream audiences. By the mideighties, however, MTV was acting much more like a radio station in business and formatting practices. Majors soon realized the promotional and popular value of videos and began to contract with professional cinematographers and television directors for important artists. New videos contained more sophisticated, professional production and cost significantly more to create. Airtime was now a coveted vehicle and eclectic, low-budget videos by less mainstream artists now had stiff competition. Which video would advertisers prefer to pay for—a new one from Michael Jackson, Madonna, or Prince or one from an unknown new wave band without radio exposure? Which one would generate a larger audience? The business of rock triumphed and noncommercial music was once more relegated to the sidelines.

Charges of racism were also leveled against MTV in its early years as African-American artists received little or no airplay. Very few Black performers were successful on the AOR rock charts. When Michael Jackson hit big in 1982 (and "Billie Jean" and "Beat It" dominated the *Billboard* charts in 1983), MTV was able to point to Jackson's videos in rebuttal. It wasn't until the significant crossover success of rap in the late 1980s that MTV viewers were regularly exposed to Black music. "Yo! MTV Raps" went on the air in 1989 and became the channel's most popular show.

Clearly MTV and the many other music-video channels (such as VH-1) have succeeded, also broadcasting in Europe and Asia. The video format has had an extraordinary impact on the promotion and sale of product. Recognizing the success and impact of music television, major labels have begun to release artist videos for sale. In 1988 no music video sales category existed in the annual Record Industry Association of America (RIAA) sales report. Six years later the 1994 report showed that 11.2 million music videos were sold for $213 million (an average price of $21 per video). We are now into our second MTV generation. Instead of doing homework to radio these kids sit in front of the television, plugged into the audio-visual excitement of MTV. . . .

Bruce Springsteen and the E Street Band

One of the most politically active major rock/pop artists of the seventies and eighties was Bruce Springsteen. The son of a bus driver and hailing from Freehold, near the New Jersey shore, his songs—depicting young people as they struggled in the small-town decay of the American dream—resonated throughout the land. Having paid his dues as a guitarist and singer in rock bands, Springsteen walked into the office of John Hammond Sr.—the man who had brought Billie Holliday, Miles Davis, Aretha Franklin, and [Bob] Dylan to Columbia Records—and, strumming an acoustic guitar, sang his American parables. The Boss's two 1973 albums, *Greetings from Asbury Park, N.J.* and *The Wild, the Innocent and the E Street Shuffle*, display a Dylanesque stream of lyrical stories. Many were driven by what would become the ultimate rock and roll band—the E Street Band: drums, bass, two guitars, two keyboards, and the R&B flavoring of Clarence Clemons on tenor sax. In 1974 *Rolling Stone* editor Jon Landau pronounced to the world this now-famous prediction: "I saw rock and roll's future and its name is Bruce Springsteen."

With the release of his classic *Born to Run* in 1975, Springsteen's stories of yearning, escape, and reflection reached the musical mainstream. In concert the E Street Band would power through an emotional three-hour journey, led by the nonstop Springsteen. The man who listened to Buddy Holly every night before he went on and paid his dues playing Jimi Hendrix covers in the sixties was viewed as a grandson of the earlier genre, delivering authentic rock and roll to the next generation of disciples. *Born to Run* went to #3 and the Boss appeared on the cover of both *Time* and *Newsweek*. A contractual wrangle with his former manager kept Springsteen out of the limelight for three years, however his 1980 #1 *The River* and the acoustic *Nebraska* sold well.

In the summer of 1984, when Springsteen was popular but not quite a superstar, he released *Born in the U.S.A.*, complete with American flag imagery on the cover. It went to #1 for seven weeks, stayed on the top-40 album charts for nearly two years, and produced seven top-10 singles, including "Dancing in the Dark," "Glory Days," and the poignant "My Hometown." The title cut, "Born in the U.S.A," describes the story of dead-end working-class life in America. The singer's brother goes to Vietnam, marries there, and is killed, and the singer, a veteran who comes home and can't get a job, wails the agonized and cynical "Born in the U.S.A." refrain. President Reagan once cited the song during a self-serving appeal to voters, and Springsteen was forced to rebut Reagan from the stage. He backed up his actions by donating money from concert proceeds to local food banks, veterans groups, the homeless, and activist trade-union groups. Springsteen continues into the nineties with only a few releases, some political activity, and a focus on his family.

Michael Jackson's Influence on Pop

Michael Jackson's solo career spanned the same twenty years as the Boss's; his live shows were also important to his popular success. In Jackson's case, however, it was his use of a video representation of live performance, dance, and story, that cemented his place as one of the megastars of the eighties. While still a member of the Jackson 5, Michael began to record solo albums, beginning with *Got to Be There* in 1972. A child star of extraordinary talent and charisma in the Frankie Lymon/Stevie Wonder tradition, Michael had performed since age five and had his first #1 hit at eleven. His solo career was unextraordinary until he began working with producer and arranger Quincy Jones; the team released *Off the Wall* (#3, September 1979) and *Thriller* (#1, December 1982), the biggest-selling album in history at over 40 million copies.

Thriller was the perfect package for the rock/pop mainstream: a talented songwriter and storyteller; a sufficiently accomplished and innovative dancer who created a dance style combining images of hip-hop, Broadway, and disco (including the moonwalk); beat-driven music; a combination of up-tempo dance songs and ballads; and guest appearances by contemporary stars Paul McCartney ("The Girl Is Mine") and Eddie Van Halen (guitar solo on "Beat It"). Jackson's use of video as a promotional tool, his conceptualization of short stories, and his focus on quality (he hired director John Landis for the "Thriller" video and shot all three videos in 35mm film) helped to solidify this album as one of the defining popular music moments of the eighties.

The quest to top an artistic and commercial success like *Thriller* usually ends in frustration and disillusionment for the artist. There is no place higher to go, especially when megastardom is achieved at age twenty-four. Two solid releases *(Bad* and *Dangerous)* followed, but the interest in Jackson in the nineties ran more toward personal history than musical accomplishment. Questions about plastic surgeries that changed his negroid features to caucasian; his man-child persona (living on an estate called Neverland surrounded by animals), and his marriage to Elvis's only child, Lisa Marie, persisted. It is difficult to say whether Michael Jackson's music will endure. It is clear, however, that Michael Jackson was the driving force behind many of the most important popular culture moments of the eighties.

Madonna Challenges Mainstream Sexual Values

Madonna was another artist who ascended to megastardom during this period. Unlike Jackson, Madonna's popularity reflected less her particular synthesis of disco, funk, and hip-hop than how she challenged the mainstream on issues of race, gender, sexual activity, sexual orientation, and power. Like Jackson, Madonna understood the power of creative music video to promote both product and artist. And through the creative and intelligent use of video, radio, television, magazines, movies, and books, Madonna presented the world with such a spectrum of images that she was able to appeal to different audiences.

Madonna Louise Ciccone was born in 1958, grew up in suburban Detroit, found her way briefly to the University of Michigan to study dance. After additional study and employment as a dancer, she immersed herself in the dance club scene of New York and released her self-titled first album in 1983. Along with her next two releases, *Like a Virgin* (#1, December 1984) and *True Blue* (#1, July 1986), also rose Madonna the artist and cultural commentator. The singles and videos from these albums offered the opportunity for the public to experience a series of contradictions. Madonna appears in *Like a Virgin* in a white bridal gown, but her movements are sexual. Who is she, a virgin or a whore? Was she Marilyn Monroe? Was her concert attire that of a slut or the redefinition of fashion and sexual power?

"Papa Don't Preach" also presented audiences with contested moral terrain. The singer tells her father she is pregnant by her boyfriend; she is determined to keep the baby but asks the father's blessing. At the same time, Madonna achieved critical acclaim in her first major movie role as a bohemian character afloat in Lower Manhattan in *Desperately Seeking Susan* (1985). Ever the cultural antagonist, Madonna's video for the 1989 title cut from *Like a Prayer* took on the issues of religion, race, and eroticism as a white woman in love with a Black saint-man. In the 1990 video "Justify My Love," Madonna and her boyfriend, Tony Ward, acted out sexual fantasies, including heterosexual sex, bisexuality, and bondage. While moral critics screamed for crucifixion, Madonna signed a services contract with Time-Warner for a reported $60 million.

Heavy Metal Matures

At the same time the pop megastars topped the charts, heavy metal's fourth generation was born. Together, hard rock/metal styles achieved sufficient commercial success to lay claim to being the most popular rock genre of the decade. This guitar-based power rock—the first generation was the Who, Cream, and [Jimi] Hendrix, the second generation Led Zeppelin—developed a third style called heavy metal in the late seventies. Though initially a cult style, metal matured and broadened its appeal in the eighties. By 1989 *Rolling Stone* magazine had announced that heavy metal was in the mainstream of rock and roll.

Back in the 1970s the audience for early metal was most often young, white, alienated, working-class male teens, who embraced a music that offered an identity and image of power, intensity, spectacle, and danger. Some observers have maintained that the difference between a Boston-Foreigner fan (hard rock) and an Iron Maiden-Judas Priest fan (heavy metal) is that the former had a life and lived with the music, whereas the latter didn't have a life and lived for the music. By the mideighties the audience for heavy metal had expanded to include preteens, those in their late twenties, and some from the middle class.

The early metal ensemble consisted of drums, bass, and one or two guitars. In the mideighties bands like Van Halen added keyboard and synthesizer, broadening both their sound and appeal. The earlier rhythm section best reflected the Zeppelin model—solid, simple, and at times lumbering. Later on, responding to punk and classical influences, rhythm players cranked it up a couple notches in speed, thus requiring better technique. Though the guitarist shared the spotlight with the vocalist, the guitar solo remained the musical highlight. It evidenced roots in both the blues, using bent notes and repetition, and also the classical tradition, with classical music guitar technique, song structure, and arpeggiated chords and phrases. The lead vocalist drew some moves and energy from earlier hard rock performers but also adopted shock stance from punk and dress and entertainment from glam (an early-1970s rock style dominated by the so-called glitter bands, such as the New York Dolls).

Heavy metal evolved in England and the United States simultaneously. England's Black Sabbath, with lead singer Ozzy Ozbourne's wails and growls, provided an early image of death, demons, and the occult. Ozbourne left to go solo in 1978, importing American guitar wizard Randy Rhoads from Quiet Riot and employing various gruesome actions as a part of his stage show. Noted for images of animal mutilation during shows, legend has it that Ozbourne had to undergo painful rabies shots when he bit the head off a bat thrown from the audience. Rhodes died in a plane crash in 1982.

Judas Priest added a second guitar to its lineup in the midseventies, speeded up the songs, and became known for its biker look and leather theatricality. Iron Maiden, named for a medieval instrument of torture, continued the themes of gloom and doom along with images of the anti-Christ, as on their *Number of the Beast* album (1982). Def Leppard paid close attention to studio details and used keyboards and special effects to move closer to the musical mainstream and increased commercial success.

In the United States, Van Halen released its self-titled first album in 1978—produced by Kiss's Gene Simmons—and by the mideighties had a #1 single, "Jump" (1985), and #1 album, *5150* (1986). David Lee Roth flaunted his showmanship and ego as frontman, but it was Eddie Van Halen, the guitarist and composer, who drove the band. Eddie reinvented metal-guitar virtuosity, using superior dexterity, speed, and a two-hand hammer/harmonic technique on the fretboard that challenged and awed all other contemporaries. With "Eruption," the second cut on the first Van Halen album, Eddie served notice of his arrival. Robert Walser maintains that Van Halen's classical music training as a pianist and violinist and his study of music theory were instrumental to this success. The education and advanced technique was reflected in the facility, fluidity, and musicianship that Eddie demonstrated as composer and guitarist. (He even quotes violin etudes in the "Eruption" solo.)

Los Angeles was also the base for other American bands, like Mötley Crüe, Quiet Riot, and later Guns 'n' Roses, whose 1987 release, *Appetite for Destruction,* was hailed as a blend of old hard rock boogie and the deep emotionality of the blues. Lead singer Axl Rose drew praise from fans for his performance style, nihilistic authenticity, and vocal wail. At the same time, however, he was criticized for lyrics and remarks that put down gays, women, African-Americans, and immigrants. . . .

Heavy Metal in Historical Context

Many mainstream critics describe heavy metal music as unidimensional, artistically impoverished, vacant, and deviant. Though the level of musicianship varies in any style, it is clear that some metal musicians and composers are among the most accomplished of any rock/pop genre. In addition, some critics don't understand audience attraction to heavy metal music, painting it as a style imposed upon youth by artists and the music industry. These critics posit that if they could only censor it or, even better, make it disappear, the problems of teens would go away.

Scholar Robert Walser addresses some of those criticisms by placing the music in its historical context: "The context . . . is the United States during the 1970s and 1980s, a period that saw a series of damaging economic crises, unprecedented corruptions of political leadership, erosion of public confidence in governmental and corporate benevolence, cruel retrenchment of social programs along with policies that favored the wealthy, and tempestuous contestations of social institutions and representations, involving formations that were thought to be stable, such as gender roles and family."[1] With society's social and economic institutions, including family relationships and the educational system, faltering and the number of family-sustaining jobs disappearing, it was natural for a style of popular music to reflect the disillusionment, fear, and powerlessness that accompanied those conditions. Male teens look for identities of power, and early metal was male and powerful. There are still bands that appeal to that particular segment of the population, and with the broadening of stylistic characteristics such as increased tempo, less morbid lyrics, and stunning guitar virtuosity combined with existent performance theatricality and driving beat, hard rock/heavy metal maintains a place in the nineties mainstream.

The Birth of Rap Music

Rap is another style that began as the soundtrack of a marginal musical community and has come to greatly influence the American musical mainstream. Rap lyrically reflects roots in the African, African-American, and Caribbean cultural traditions of "playing the dozens," "signifying," the griot tradition of reporting and praise, and also "toasting" and "dub" from Jamaican sound-system DJs. These expressive forms contributed boasting, praise, mockery, and storytelling to the genre. Musically, rap derived from jazz improvisations and avant-garde musical essentialism, social commentary of the blues and rhythm and blues, and the syncopated soul and funk sounds of James Brown and others from the seventies.

These influences combined during the mid-1970s in New York's South Bronx, with its neighborhoods dominated by crumbling housing and its lack of economic opportunity for citizens. Rising from this environment of urban decay was the multiethnic culture called hip-hop, a phenomenon that created a source of identity and group affiliation in "crews"—such as DJ Afrika Bambaataa's Zulu Nation—and acted as an alternative to gang warfare. This hip-hop culture spawned dress styles, break dancing, graffiti, and rap music.

Initially modeling themselves after the Jamaican mobile sound-system DJs, early rap DJs would play at indoor dance clubs or tap into power from a city lamppost and set up an outdoors dance. DJ Kool Herc, a Jamaican living in New York, is credited with numerous innovations that led to rap. With his monster speakers (named Herculords), Herc extended the instrumental breaks from selections to such an extent that dancers would seize the time to demonstrate their latest steps. As Tricia Rose describes in her outstanding book on rap, these "break-dancers" would take ten to thirty seconds to show off their latest acrobatic steps and pantomime moves. The DJs soon began inviting the dancers to the local dance clubs where the DJs worked. DJ Kool Herc would sometimes recite rhymes along with these breaks.

Grand Master Flash was another South Bronx DJ and pioneer who is credited with popularizing scratching, and thus the use of the turntable as an instrument. He would manually turn a record back and forth under the needle, causing a scratching sound to provide rhythmic accents and syncopation. Flash, after attaching a microphone to his system, invited friends Melle Mel and Cowboy to rap along with him. As rappers began to display lyrical and rhythmic talent they became entertainers along with, and then eventually superseded, the dancers. Rap crews like Grand Master Flash and the Furious Five were formed alongside the already existing dance and graffiti crews.

A small New Jersey label, Sugar Hill Records, capitalized on this new sound, releasing "Rapper's Delight" in 1979. Over a disco track lifted from the group Chic, the Sugar Hill Gang introduced rap to the musical mainstream. In spite of criticism from the 'hood that the record's rap was plastic, it eventually sold over 10 million copies worldwide and made the top-40 charts at #36. In 1982 Grand Master Flash and the Furious Five released "The Message," a song chronicling the hardships of life in the neighborhood. Jon Schecter, in the liner notes to the 1992 Rhino release *Street Jams*, calls it an "epic poem of the urban landscape." In the refrain, in response to the litany of struggles, the rapper decries, "It's like a jungle sometimes, makes me wonder, how I keep from goin' under."

Rap Enters the Mainstream

Rap musicians had a steady stream of releases on independent labels like Tommy Boy, Profile, and Def Jam through the mideighties. In 1986 Run-DMC, three Queens rappers, had a #4 hit with their remake of the Aerosmith song "Walk This Way."[2] Critics cited the unique use of rock music samples, including some of the original guitar and vocals, but Tricia Rose notes that rappers had been appropriating a variety of musics in their genre for years.[3] From this point in time, with the tremendous media exposure of Run-DMC, rap entered mainstream consciousness. A white New York group, the Beastie Boys, followed the next year with "(You Gotta) Fight for the Right (to Party)" (#7, January 1987). The same year, Queens rapper L.L. Cool J (for Ladies Love Cool James) had the first of his five top-40 hits, "I Need Love."

Rap artists emerged from other African-American communities. Gangsta rap was a new subgenre with commentaries on urban life in Los Angeles, gangs in the community, ordinary citizens in danger, and a police force viewed as perpetrators of violence. Ice T was its first popular voice and had a hit album, *Power,* in 1988. On his 1992 album *Body Count* the cut "Cop Killer" contained the lyric "dust off" some cops and his record company, under public pressure, removed the song from subsequent releases.

N.W.A. (Niggas With Attitudes) profiled struggles in the L.A. ghetto of Compton much the same way Grand Master Flash had done for the Bronx earlier in the decade. Their 1989 release, *Straight Outta Compton* (#37, April 1989), was described as "graphic, lurid streetscapes" and included the single, "F—k the Police." Set as a courtroom trial of the police, the cut charged that the police "think they have authority to kill the minority" and "thinkin' every nigga sellin' narcotic." A "gangsta" was a tough talking, streetwise, expletive-hurling Black man, and the album earned N.W.A. a warning from the F.B.I. Like white working-class youth finding power in the heavy metal identity, it is easy to see how disenfranchised Black youth could concur with these macho expressions of power and bravado. It is also clear that rap's characterization of American society as oppressive and unfriendly found support across broad segments of the African-American community.

Back on the East Coast, Public Enemy released its second album, *It Takes a Nation of Millions to Hold Us Back,* in 1988. Evident were not only the illuminating Black power sermons of "Bring the Noise," "Party for Your Right to Fight," and "Prophets of Rage," but also the brilliant collage of samples, sounds, and beats driving the message. This musical maturing of the rap style manifests itself in a more sophisticated use of samples to layer multitimbral, rhythmic elements behind Malcolm X speeches and guitar solos by Living Color's Vernon Reid. Public Enemy continues its tradition of strident commentary on the hypocrisy and injustices of American society into the nineties. . . .

Rap has had a significant impact on American popular

music, not because we find other musicians emulating the style, but because it expresses a clear and direct relationship between popular music and the struggles involved in an increasingly problematic everyday life. In addition, its strident tone has called upon Americans to again consider the continuing struggles of the African-American community. As Tricia Rose explains, "African-American musicians find a way to unnerve and simultaneously revitalize American culture."[4]

1. Robert Walser, *Running with the Devil: Power, Gender, and Madness in Heavy Metal* Music (Hanover, N.H.: Wesleyan University Press, 1993), p. xvii.

2. "MC" is a hip-hop term for "mic controller."

3. See Tricia Rose, *Black Noise: Rap Music and Black Culture in Contemporary America* (Hanover, N.H.: Wesleyan University Press, 1994).

4. Ibid., p. 188.

The "Yuppie" Phenomenon Is Reflected on Film

William J. Palmer

Many social commentators have characterized the 1980s as a decade of materialism and greed. However accurate or inaccurate this generalization may be, the popular media of the 1980s was concerned with the supposed emergence of a new class of "yuppies" (young urban professionals): Men and women, mostly white and aged between twenty and forty, whose primary characteristic was an obsession with financial success. As William J. Palmer explains in the following selection, "yuppie-ism" was a popular subject for movies in the 1980s. Palmer, an English professor and the author of *The Films of the Eighties: A Social History*, suggests that the portrayal of yuppies in the films of the 1980s reflects society's growing unease with the materialistic aspects of American culture.

In the action comedy *Burglar* (1987), Whoopie Goldberg and Bob Goldthwaite steel themselves to enter a crowded fern bar to gather information, when Goldthwaite panics and babble-screams: "I can't go in there! I can't go in there! It's full of crazed yuppies from hell!" While the Hell's Angels of the biker films of the fifties and early sixties have not really been replaced by the Hell's yuppies of the eighties, Goldthwaite's terror at the spector of America's cities being taken over by roving gangs of young urban professionals wearing three-piece suits, driving Volvos, BMWs, and Mercedes, and flaunting their Gold Card wealth in an orgy of material acquisitiveness certainly seemed the case in the films of the eighties.

A Sign of the Times

Residing at the opposite end of the spectrum from the Mid-American, rural, feminism of the farm crisis films, the text of urban yuppie materialism also exhibited a neoconservative style fostered by Reagonomics. The yuppie drives to make large amounts of money quickly, to succeed in a ruthless competitive world, to acquire the most expensive material goods, to spend rather than save, to party extremely hard as a reward for working extremely hard, to sacrifice (especially human relationships) for one's job, mirrored the Reagan administration's deficit spending policies and hi-tech defense system acquisitions. Eighties yuppies saw their ruthless competitive work ethic and their consumptive materialism as hedges and buffers against an increasingly unstable terrorist- and nuclear- and deficit-threatened world. Yuppieness became a form of protective coloration against the economic and status threats from ethnic minorities and the poor, from a questionable national economy, from an increasingly competitive world. Yuppies saw themselves as a uniformed cavalry circling the wagons around what was left of the American dream, that dream's material icons: the job with a chance for advancement, the house (in its new condo form), the car, the status goods, perhaps even a controlled and economically justified family. The films of the eighties were acutely aware not only of the stereotypes and accoutrements of the yuppie lifestyle but also of the insecurity of the dying American dream.

For example, in the eighties, the heroes of films were less likely to be cowboys or spacemen with the right stuff or loner cops like Dirty Harry Callahan (Clint Eastwood) than they were businessmen or marketing executives or advertising geniuses. In films like *Kramer vs. Kramer* (1979),

Nothing in Common (1986), *Baby Boom* (1986), *Planes, Trains and Automobiles* (1987), *The Secret of My Success* (1987), *Parenthood* (1989), *When Harry Met Sally,* and *Crazy People* (1990), the central characters are all advertising executives, while in *Wall Street* (1987), *Dad* (1989), and *Rollover* (1981), the central characters are all aggressive urban money men. . . .

In eighties films, the characters were more likely to inhabit the milieu and the economic strata of the yuppie than any other segment of the American public.

Yuppie Angst

The major eighties document, in both its novel and film forms, of yuppie angst was Jay McInerney's 1984 best seller and film adaptation *Bright Lights, Big City* (1988). . . .

Bright Lights, Big City is a declawed eighties version of *Dr. Jekyll and Mr. Hyde.* See cute little conservative materialistic Alex Keaton (also Michael J. Fox) of the long-running eighties TV sitcom "Family Ties" turn into guilty, confused cokehead and undersized playboy of the New York disco scene. Jamie's friend Ted Allegash (Kiefer Sutherland) describes their dark yuppie Hyde-like quest: "Into the heart of the night. Wherever there are dances to be danced, drugs to be hoovered, girls to be Allegashed.". . .

But *Bright Lights, Big City* also provides a checklist of the yuppie image. It defines the uniform—button-down shirt, tie, three-piece suit—or more casually—shirt, tie, sports jacket, jeans—and, of course, no self-respecting yuppie ever sleeps in anything but an Ivy League T-shirt—Jamie is a Dartmouth grad. The yuppie uniform is this confused mix of the formal and the casual; Dustin Hoffman wore it in *Kramer vs. Kramer* (1979), Michael Murphy in *Manhattan* (1979), and Steve Martin in *Roxanne* (1987). Drugs serve as the anaesthetic to the confusion of this life; they create the illusion that all of this imagery means something.

One other early eighties film, Lawrence Kasdan's *Big Chill* (1983) presented the same sort of angst-burdened blueprint of the yuppie lifestyle. Late in that film, Meg's

(Mary Kay Place) best friend, Sarah (Glenn Close), in an act of generosity has just sent her husband, Harold (Kevin Kline), in to impregnate Meg with the baby Meg so wants. Despite her delight at this turn of events, Meg confesses "I feel like I just got a great deal on a used car!" Meg's feeling could serve as a metaphor for the yuppie eighties. The decade seems to be a nostalgic attempt to regain the innocent acquisitive joy of the American dream of the fifties and the passion of the sixties while simultaneously realizing that the dream is rusted out and has too many miles on it. All of the characters in *The Big Chill* have pretty much gotten the deal they wanted but it has not worked out.

The film begins at Alex's funeral. A member of a close-knit group of friends who all went to college at Michigan in the late sixties, Alex has committed suicide. During the funeral, the preacher ironically asks the film's thematic question: "Where did Alex's hope go?" But the question applies to this whole generation who in the years since the fiery radicalism of their college days have chilled out.

Like *Bright Lights, Big City, The Big Chill* is a checklist film for the yuppie generation, but it carries the extra baggage of comparing the eighties yuppies to their past sixties selves before the big chill set in. That change, from a passionate and involved sixties generation to the cool and aloof yuppie generation, is endlessly dissected in a weekend of soul-searching triggered by Alex's suicide. His death, the first of their generation going to the big sleep because of the big chill of the mindless acquisitive Reagan eighties, is an intrusion upon all of these people's nice safe yuppie lives. . . .

The Job Battle

Most often, the workplace became the yuppie battlefield. Their jobs took precedence over all other areas of their lives: self, relationships, family, morality. The competition for success, power, status, money, in the workplace and in society became an unhealthy obsession. . . .

Wall Street (1987) is the ultimate film text of the workplace battlefield. It inventories the ammunition that loads up the yuppie dream, tracks the quick and easy money that fires that dream off. In *Wall Street,* Gordon Gekko (Michael Douglas), microphone in hand and working the room like a rock star, addresses a corporate stockholders' meeting and delivers the Gettysburg Address of the yuppie philosophy:

> Well, ladies and gentlemen, we're not here to indulge in fantasy, but in political and economic reality. America, America has become a second rate power. Its trade deficit and its fiscal deficit are at nightmare proportions. . . . Today, management has no stake in the company. . . . *You* own the company and you are being royally screwed over. . . . Well in my book you either do it right or you get eliminated. In the last seven deals that I have been involved with, there were 2.5 million stockholders who have made a pre-tax profit of 12 billion dollars. [applause] Thank you. I am not a destroyer of companies; I am a liberator of them. The point is, ladies and gentlemen, that greed, for lack of a better word, greed is good. Greed is right. Greed works. Greed clarifies, cuts through and captures the essence of the evolutionary spirit. Greed, in all its forms, greed for life, for money, for love, for knowledge, has marked the upward surge of mankind and, greed, you mark my words, will not only save Teldar Paper, but that other malfunctioning corporation called the USA. Thank you very much.

Gekko's speech, his preposterous paean to greed, rings with a kind of evangelistic fervor. . . . Greed, literally, becomes a savior for . . . the USA, and Gekko's speech becomes a fervent absolution of the yuppie angst that clouds the hardhearted decision making of corporate raiding.

Wall Street is the ultimate yuppie nightmare. It portrays the crash of the yuppie ideal of money, power, and status. . . .

Buddy Fox (Charlie Sheen) is an American innocent from Queens who has worked his way into the inner circle of stock brokerage trading, hostile takeover deals, and the Manhattan yuppie ratrace. It is no wonder that his father Carl (Martin Sheen), the representative of an airplane mechanic's union, has nicknamed him Huckleberry. By a lot of toadying, Buddy becomes the protégé and soon-to-be fall guy for Gordon Gekko, the most ruthless of the *Wall Street* corporate raiders. To use the metaphoric language of actual corporate raiding, the plot of Wall Street is like a medieval joust. Gekko, the black knight, and Sir Laurence Wildman (Terence Stamp), the white knight, fight it out with telephones mounted on stretch limos attended by their squires who are either Brooks Brothers lawyers or innocent young stockbrokers like Fox. . . .

Gordon Gekko relishes his macho battle rhetoric, but Bud Fox is defined in terms of a more human metaphor, that of sex. In the world of *Wall Street,* the human emotions of love and the excitement and release of sexuality are overshadowed by the making of money. Making money becomes a twisted form of sex, an almost orgasmic thrill. After buying a painting for $2.5 million, Gekko invites Darien (Darryl Hannah), Bud's upscale decorator girl friend, to share a room at the Carlyle Hotel for the afternoon. "You and I are the same, Darien," Gekko argues. "We are smart enough not to buy into the oldest myth running, love—a fiction created by people to keep them from jumping out of windows.". . .

The yuppie dream is based solely upon making money and owning things, on wearing the uniform at a young age while it still fits. The only problem is that when they attain the dream they find it empty. That is why, after a perfect dinner cooked with the help of every possible yuppie kitchen appliance in his perfect apartment, and after perfect sex with a perfect woman, Bud Fox finds himself out on his balcony looking at the city skyline and asking, "Who am I?" The ultimate nightmare of the yuppie dream is that one must give up all that they are to attain it. . . .

The Religion of Acquisition

If the yuppie characters of films like *Wall Street* and *The Secret of My Success* are obsessed with making money, they are equally driven to spend it. Acquiring the most expensive components of the uniform, whether it be clothes or cars or homes or art or power over others, became a sole form of nonworking-hours entertainment pursued with an almost religious zeal. Second only to their love of working is the yuppies' love of shopping. This religion of acquisition's Rome is Fifth Avenue in New York and its Mecca is Rodeo Drive in L.A., and all its parishes and sects are located in the malls and designer specialty shops and luxury car dealers all across America.

Another group of films, not satisfied with satirizing this yuppie religion of acquisition, examined the consequences of the obsession with money. In *Prizzi's Honor* (1985), money wins out over love as husband and wife hitpersons choose to accept contracts on each other rather than give up either their money or their earned status. Charlie Partanna (Jack Nicholson) is a corporate executive in one of America's most profitable companies, organized crime. Irene Walker (Kathleen Turner) is a freelance broker, a cold, accountantlike hitwoman who wears the yuppie uniform from her Excalibur car to her designer clothes to her upscale California home. The clear passion that these two feel for each other, however, cannot compete with their tenacity for holding their money and status. This yuppie irony of love turning to violence over possession surfaces again in *The War of the Roses* (1989).

Another plot that explores the consequences arising from the religion of acquisition is the "sins of the fathers." This plot motivates action in both *The Breakfast Club* (1985) and *Say Anything* (1989), two of the more serious of the hundreds of teen problem films of the eighties. *The Breakfast Club* dissects the defenses that an encounter group of teenagers in a suburban high school, all of whom have yuppie parents more interested in money and acquisition than in them, have built up around themselves in order to cope with a world that seems to have opted for a strict caste system based upon money and style. *Say Anything* is an offbeat teenage love story in which Lloyd Dobler (John Cusack), an extremely ordinary young man, pursues and actually wins Diane Cort (Ione Skye), who is not only gorgeous but is also the class valedictorian and has won the most prestigious college scholarship in America. In its teen love plot, *Say Anything* is an utterly conventional film, but its subplot concerning Diane's nice yuppie father embezzling hundreds of thousands of dollars from his nursing home patients is what proves the major obstacle to Lloyd and Diane's love relationship.

One other set of films, perhaps best represented by *Risky Business* (1983), *Sixteen Candles* (1984), and *Ferris Bueller's Day Off* (1986), portray the rebellion of the eighties teen generation against their yuppie parents' attitudes and things. The major tragedies in these films are yuppie tragedies such as the repeated crashing of a father's expensive sports car. In *Risky Business,* the sports car goes into a lake; in *Ferris Bueller's Day Off*, it crashes through the back of its cantilevered garage and over the side of a cliff. With their yuppie parents too caught up in materialistic obsessions and job ambitions, these neglected teens get attention by trashing their parents' uniform and all its accessories.

Yuppie Relationships

Can Yuppies Maintain Sexual Relationships? That depends, but even when they manage to establish relationships it is a real struggle. Perhaps the single most frightening bugaboo of the yuppie lifestyle is the specter of involvement. That scary spook haunts the title characters in *When Harry Met Sally* (1989). They are yuppies to their eyebrows, and the film tracks their relationship over twelve years—1977 to 1989—in New York. In a sense, *When Harry Met Sally* is a social history of this single issue—fear of relationships—across the whole yuppie era.

Harry is a fast-talking, witty advertising man, while Sally (Meg Ryan) is an emotional, picky, highly ironic careerwoman. The film focuses upon their talk—in cars, in restaurants, in airplanes, in Central Park, on the telephone in separate beds—about the ironies of yuppie sexual insecurity. Each generation has its own version of this film—in the fifties it was *Pillow Talk* (1959); in the sixties Audrey

Hepburn and Albert Finney were *Two for the Road* (1967); for the seventies it was Barbra Streisand and Robert Redford analyzing *The Way We Were* (1973)—and *When Harry Met Sally* is the eighties decade's romantic chronicle. Laughing at the byzantine intricacies of yuppie insecurities, *When Harry Met Sally* is about the difference between friendship and relationship. Of course, the difference is sex. The film fixates on twelve years of a single couple trying to sort out the stresses of being friends or lovers or both. If they are representative of the yuppie generation, then it is a miracle that the concept of marriage still exists and celibacy is not universal. It is no coincidence that the funniest scene in the film is a faked orgasm. The film is about coitus interruptus, about sacrificing an inner life for an outer life of simulation and show. . . .

St. Elmo's Fire (1985) provides a rogue's gallery of interpersonally screwed-up yuppies. How can these Georgetown graduates have been so successful in their studies and in their new jobs, yet be so terribly confused in their personal lives? Alex (Judd Nelson) is a ruthless congressional aide and Kirbo (Emilio Estevez) is a law student, but both, in the presence of women they are trying to impress, make complete fools of themselves. Billy (Rob Lowe), a talented sax player, has exactly the opposite problem. Though he is married and has a child, he still chases women and flees the commitment of his family. Kevin (Andrew McCarthy) is a would-be writer whose Byronic poutiness covers his insecurities. The women in this rogue's gallery are no less yuppie and no more stable than the men. Wendy (Mare Willingham) is a Washington, D.C., welfare worker, but she must be a rigorously sheltered one because she falls for the narcissistic self-absorption of Billy. Leslie (Ally Sheedy), an architect, is smart enough to see through the utterly dishonest Alex but falls for the moody Kevin. The most self-deceived is Jules (Demi Moore) whose cocaine habit turns her into "a sad and funny Yuppie slut."[1] Ultimately, *St. Elmo's Fire* is about the paralyzing insecurity that these otherwise decisive, intelligent, and successful young professionals feel in their private lives. . . .

Like so many other aspects of the yuppie lifestyle as portrayed in the films of the eighties, the issue of whether that fast-paced, high-pressure, materially obsessed public lifestyle allows for a private life of human relationship was plagued by self-doubts, guilts, and indecisiveness. Within both love relationships and family relationships, doubt was consistently raised as to the yuppy's ability to redirect his or her energies from the public lifestyle to the private life.

Can Yuppies Have Babies? Eventually they can, after they get the job and acquire the uniform and manage to overcome their fear of commitment. If 1987 was the year of the Vietnam War films, and 1984 was the year of the farm crisis films, then 1987-88 was certainly the year of the yuppie baby, both in American society and in films. The National Center for Health in 1988 released statistics indicating that 3.8 million babies were born in 1987, the largest number of births since 1964. "Parents are facing the biological clock," National Institute of Child Health population analyst Arthur Campbell speculated. But if there was a significant baby boom in society, there was also one in the films of the last three years of the decade. From *Raising Arizona* (1987) to *Baby Boom* (1987) to *Made in Heaven* (1987) to *Three Men and a Baby* (1987) to *She's Having a Baby* (1987) to *For Keeps* (1988) to *Big Business* (1988) to *Look Who's Talking* (1989), babies proved the most popular props available. . . .

One of the final yuppie baby films of the eighties, *Look Who's Talking* (1989), in its central point of view, makes one of the funniest yet most universal comments upon not only the yuppie lifestyle but all of these other yuppie films. *Look Who's Talking* is a continuously self-reflexive film in which a single observer inside the film comments ironically, comically, upon the events and the world of the film. That observer just happens to be a baby and the self-reflexiveness of his critique of the eighties world into which he is born could serve as a metaphor for what is happening in every yuppie film of the decade. Consistently this competitive materialist lifestyle is questioned and critiqued. Every yuppie film, whether a social drama like *Wall Street,* a weepy like *Immediate Family,* a political film like *True Believer,* or one of the hundreds of yuppie comedies, turned on the idea that yuppies were finding out that though they made a lot of money and owned a lot of nice things, they were still coming up empty-handed as human beings.

1. Jack Kroll, "Hollywood's Lost Lambkins," *Newsweek,* 1 July 1985, 55.

America Struggles with the Legacy of Vietnam

Pat Aufderheide

Historians agree that the Vietnam War—in the eyes of many, the first conflict that America ever lost—has had a profound effect on America's national character. In the following selection, Pat Aufderheide, a professor of communication at American University and an editor of the magazines *In These Times* and *Black Film Review*, examines how Americans' changing perceptions of Vietnam were reflected in popular culture. In her view, the construction of the Vietnam War Memorial in 1982 marked Americans' first willingness to publicly deal with the war. The 1985 blockbuster *Rambo*, in which the hero returns to Vietnam—and is, this time, successful—resonated with many Americans' beliefs about how the war should have been conducted. Finally, says Aufderheide, the 1986 film *Platoon*, along with a host of late-'80s films that portrayed the conflict in a more emotional light, reflected the growing perception of the Vietnam War as a national tragedy from which America was only beginning to recover.

R ain or shine, weekday or weekend, they file into the trough of the Vietnam Memorial in Washington, D.C. They emerge somber and shaken from this monument to

Excerpted and edited from "Vietnam: Good Soldiers," by Pat Aufderheide, in *Seeing Through Movies*, edited by Mark Crispin Miller (New York: Pantheon). Copyright ©1990 by Pat Aufderheide. Reprinted with permission from the author. The full version of this article can be found in *The Daily Planet: A Critic on the Capitalist Culture Beat*, by Pat Aufderheide (Minneapolis: University of Minnesota Press, 2000).

inchoate sorrow, and there are always more behind them. Some, hoping to make a connection, leave behind mementos; more than 12,000 personal objects left there are now archived in perpetuity. Nothing better symbolizes how Vietnam has hovered in the American popular consciousness—unavoidable but inexplicable, a horror to be grasped only at the level of adding up the dead one by one.

Acknowledging Vietnam

It took Americans until 1982 to erect a monument to the Vietnam War. It took longer still for the makers of American movies and television programs—those avenues through which history becomes part of popular consciousness—to find a way to transform discordant political passions and unbearable images into entertainment. Only in the later 1980s, after periods of filmic silence and false starts, did the war become the subject of a subgenre, one that could be called the "noble-grunt film."

The noble-grunt films have been widely heralded as a sign of the maturing of the American audience—an audience finally ready for brutally frank images of the war the way it was really fought. But they are better seen as reconstructing the place of Vietnam in American popular history, away from a political process and toward an understanding of the war as a psychological watershed. Indeed, they speak more eloquently to the psychological plight of the average moviegoer today than to any reality of the war years. Just as the Vietnam Memorial enabled a public acknowledgment of personal mourning, films and TV shows of the later eighties evinced a sense of loss and a recognition of the need for grief. . . .

The Vietnam War marked a messy end point to "the American century" in popular culture. "The sixties" has become a talismanic reference to that rupture in expectations and self-image, and the sixties reevaluation that hit late-eighties media always referred to Vietnam. You could see it in the movies—for instance, in *The Big Chill,* all about people caught up in the era without having been actors in it and nostalgic about anti-war atmospherics. The film's popular reception testified that millions who were merely present in the era remained psychologically unaccounted for long afterward.

In the late eighties that very sense of confusion became the psychological center of films and TV programs about the war. Films as different as *Platoon* (1986), *Full Metal Jacket* (1987), *Good Morning, Vietnam* (1987), *Hamburger Hill* (1987), *Gardens of Stone* (1987), *84 Charlie MoPic* (1989), *Off Limits* (1988), *Dear America* (1988), *Casualties of War* (1989), and TV series like *Tour of Duty* and *China Beach* have carried into film what author C.D.B. Bryan described for literature as "the Generic Vietnam War Narrative." This generic narrative features combat units in tales that chart "the gradual deterioration of order, the disinteration of idealism, the breakdown of character, the alienation from those at home, and finally, the loss of all sensibility save the will to survive." There is something terribly sad and embattled about these films and TV shows, even in their lighter and warmer moments. They celebrate survival as a form of heroism, and cynicism as a form of self-preservation.

Good Soldiers Versus Bureaucracy

The noble-grunt films collectively recast the war as a test of physical and, much more important, psychological survival of the person who had no authority and too much responsibility. The war is seen from the viewpoint of the American soldiers in the barracks and bars, in the jungles and the paddies (rarely in the air or on water). The war is confined to the years in which the most ground troops were present. The battlefield has been internalized, and internalized, and the enemy is not so much the Vietnamese as the cold, abstract forces of bureaucracy and the incompetence of superiors. . . .

Hamburger Hill's subject, the taking of a pointless strategic objective, where soldiers suffered 70 percent casualties, carries its implicit indictment of military officers into every scene. In TV series incompetent and corrupt officers and embassy officials punctuate the hard life of the grunts and the medical and R&R staff—a seemingly bold, but contained, criticism of higher-ups. . . .

However accurate the films may be—and the battle scenes from *Platoon* and *Hamburger Hill* (directed by John Irvin, who was a BBC film director in Vietnam), among others, have won high praise—their claim implicitly goes further than telling us what some combat soldiers suffered. They claim to tell us "the real truth" and, finally, how to feel about the war. . . .

Reagan Rejects "the Vietnam Syndrome"

[In 1979] Americans . . . were being buffeted with bad news. A nation that, with an energy shortage in 1973, had been given a taste of the end of affluence now faced international humiliation when Iranian students kidnapped U.S. embassy personnel in Teheran in 1979 and held them for more than a year. "America held hostage!" blared the television sets in millions of homes. It seemed as if the specter of Nixon's "pitiful, helpless giant" had taken on flesh. Environmental crises further ate away at the image of a nation both preeminent and righteous.

When Ronald Reagan assumed office, he seized upon a reason for the precipitate decline in American prestige: "the Vietnam syndrome." More, he promised a new dawn, a morning in America. And he proceeded to conduct international affairs as if he were reading a film script, altering reality to fit needs. Nazi SS soldiers at Bitburg became "victims" as much as the concentration camp dead. The tiny island of Grenada, completing a small landing strip for tourism, became an invasion threat to the U.S. and the object of an invasion. The rantings of the bizarre dictator Muammar Qaddafi became a justification for the first overt American attempt to kill the head of another country. The Nicaraguan contra forces became freedom fighters for democracy.

No matter what the outcome—even when hundreds of Marines died in a terrorist attack on a barracks in Lebanon—Reagan personally garnered support because he resolutely played the role of ordinary American, outraged and aggrieved. The decision-maker, the power-holder, projected the attitude of a put-upon victim of decision-making. It was a brilliant psychological ploy for a president who depended on popular support while exercising policies that were often unpopular and sometimes secret.

Reagan found a movie hero to match his own public persona, one to whom he proudly compared himself: Rambo. It was an interesting choice for the powerful man who played to fantasies of righteous vengeance among those who felt themselves powerless. Rambo was the perennial righteous underdog, the survivor of alienation and rejection.

Rambo "Refights" the War and Wins

Rambo—a pre-adolescent boy with Nautilized muscles, a wounded giant in chains, who, although he breaks the chains, can never be healed—was also the figure who paved the way for public acceptance of the noble grunt. Sylvester Stallone had initially played the character in *First Blood* (1982, directed by Ted Kotcheff). John Rambo was a vet with post-Vietnam shock, who acted out the nihilistic rage of the forgotten man, among other things wasting a local police force contemptuous of war-torn vets. The first film ended downbeat, with Rambo going to prison. *Rambo*, the 1985 film directed by George Cosmatos, picked him up there, breaking rocks in a hellhole whose value for the battered and betrayed vet is that "here at least I know how I stand." And it transformed Rambo from psychotic to savior.

The plot, larded with explosive action sequences, revolves around a secret mission to find MIAs (missing in action). The choice of target is significant; the question of whether any living Americans remain in Vietnam has lingered in public consciousness as a kind of objective correlative to our lack of closure about the "Vietnamized" war. Rambo, too, is a symbol of the war's unresolved end. He's a ghost in the machine, like the MIAs. When his mentor Trautman warns him, "The old Vietnam is dead," he says,

"I'm alive, it's still alive, ain't it?" And, indeed, Rambo gets to rerun history in this movie, which allows him to refight the war alone. . . .

Rambo's ultimate triumph is as much over the corrupt bureaucrats as over the Vietnamese; after returning to base with the MIAs, his last act of violence is to machine-gun the corrupt bureaucrat's equipment and threaten his life. But even in victory Rambo is condemned to obscurity; the heroic innocent remains the victim. Rambo's guerrilla war has a special poignancy because he is the unacknowledged secret defender of American values. "All I want," he tells Trautman with choked anger at the end, "all *they* [pointing to the rescued MIAs] want, and every other guy who came

'80s Films Mirror the Ambiguities of the Times

Interestingly, the films of the 1980s point . . . to the ambiguities of Reagan's America. *Red Dawn* and *Rocky IV* celebrated American patriotism and anticommunism in a manner unthinkable in the era of Vietnam and Watergate, while films like *Top Gun* implicitly lauded American military power. "Teen" movies like *Back to the Future* had incipient yuppie heroes; the rebellious cult figures characteristic of the 1950s and 1960s were gone from the screens. On the other hand, "save-the-farm" movies, notably *Places in the Heart, Country,* and *The River,* depicted the grim plight of rural America. The materialism and greed of the new entrepreneurial culture came under critical scrutiny in *Wall Street.* Movies also offered differing views of the Vietnam War. Sylvester Stallone's Rambo films portrayed this as a good cause and attributed America's defeat to national loss of will. In contrast, *Platoon* and *Full Metal Jacket* emphasized the brutal and brutalizing aspects of the conflict.

Iwan W. Morgan, "The Age of Uncertainty: The United States Since 1973," in Iwan W. Morgan and Neil A. Wynn, eds., *America's Century: Perspectives on U.S. History Since 1900.* New York: Holmes & Meier, 1993.

over here and spilled his guts and gave everything he had wants, is for our country to love us as much as we love it."

Rambo is the tragic image of an America wounded by circumstance. Life has not been fair to Rambo, or to America. The film's legacy was not so much in its muscular action sequences—although they guaranteed it enduring international success—as in the image of a vet wronged but right.

Just how well *Rambo* fit the times was evoked when Lieutenant Colonel Oliver North testified in Congress during the Iran-contra scandal. His demeanor recalled the same petulant, self-righteous, hurt-little-boy attitude that Stallone expresses at the beginning of the film. Ollie North's behavior as a member of the National Security Council also had parallels with Rambo's. He, too, was a cowboy of foreign policy, having "learned" from Vietnam to do it right this time, demonstrating contempt for lines of authority in the name of patriotism.

Coming to Terms with the Vietnam War

The Rambo age of presidential image politics came to an end with the 1988 election. George Bush did not have the style, skill, or will to reverse, in his personal presentation, the image of power as Reagan had done so deftly. He did, however, invoke the specter of Vietnam in his inaugural address. "That war cleaves us still," he said. "Surely the statute of limitations has been reached. . . . No great nation can long afford to be sundered by a memory."

The movies, however, had already re-remembered Vietnam, in the process transforming the social cleavages to which Bush referred into smaller, far more manageable psychological ones. They had cleared the way for the next phase of reimagining the Vietnam experience on screen: the part where the vets come home. Even as Bush called for a kinder, gentler America built on local volunteerism and a rebuilding of community spirit ("a thousand points of light"), Vietnam vets in the movies had come back and were learning to live again. . . .

The process of learning to live again in the wake of the

war was . . . a hot Hollywood subject, with such projects as Oliver Stone's *Born on the Fourth of July* and Norman Jewison's *In Country*. . . .

The issue was the plight of the vet attempting, in the midst of a shattered community at home, to recover from the shattering of community in Vietnam. In films like *Heartbreak Ridge* (1986), *Distant Thunder* (1988), *Jacknife* (1989), and *In Country* (1989) the vet is the symbol of an America scrambling for its moral and psychic footing. All these films stress the pathos of the man who suffered and was scarred, who performs the heroic act of returning to life, and who calls into question the macho John Wayne image that got packed into the baggage along with the rifles in Vietnam. . . .

Born on the Fourth of July (1989) . . . raised sentimentality to a battlecry of betrayal. The crippled survivor-hero (Tom Cruise as Ron Kovic) rages against his impotence, which director Oliver Stone has said symbolizes the plight of America today. It is a fate brought on by a macho Marine recruiter, a steely commander who denies him his remorse at killing Vietnamese civilians and his own men, and most of all by a Catholic mom who sold him on simplistic patriotism. Aided by antiwar vets, Kovic finally comes "home" when he delivers a speech at the 1976 Democratic convention, although home will always be, for him, pathetic impotence in a wheelchair.

Whatever happens to them, these vets are survivors of a general breakdown of community. Their heroism lies in their choosing to forgive themselves, improvise a future, weather hostility from a few unfeeling civilians, and accept the acceptance of many others.

We are on our way, in the movies, to forgiving ourselves not for anything the U.S. government and forces did in Vietnam but simply for having felt so bad for so long. It remains to be seen whether this is a cultural landscape in which, as some hope, "we can find new determination to brave the opening expanse," or the platform on which new castles of nostalgic delusion will be built—or both. Either way, it is a profoundly personal matter rather than a political or historical one, emotionally predicated on a sense of loss and propelled by a therapeutic tone of self-help.

The Vietnam movies of the later eighties expressed and helped to shape a consensus that the event was not a war but a tragedy. This tragedy was not political, and it was certainly not shared by or with the Vietnamese. It was entirely ours—the grunts of history, the innocents, the powerless ones, the "good soldiers." The enemy was not over there but above us, somewhere in the cold regions of policy and commerce, those regions beyond the control of the consumer. We have been abandoned, these films told us, and must heat ourselves. The war is over, but the damage remains. Distrust, alienation, a loss of history, and a huddled-over sense of self-protection are our legacy.

Chronology

1980

April 24—Eight Americans die in a failed attempt to rescue hostages being held in Tehran, Iran.

November 4—Ronald Reagan is elected president.

1981

January 20—American hostages being held in Iran are released minutes after Reagan is sworn in as president.

March 30—John W. Hinckley Jr. attempts to assassinate President Reagan outside the Washington Hilton Hotel. The president is shot but quickly recovers. His press secretary, James Brady, is severely wounded, and a policeman and a Secret Service agent are also hit.

August 13—Reagan signs a major tax cut into law.

October 2—As part of a military buildup, Reagan announces plans to build B-1 bomber and MX missiles.

1982

March 31—Reagan denounces nuclear freeze movement.

June 12—A massive nuclear freeze demonstration takes place in New York City.

November 10—Soviet leader Leonid Brezhnev dies and is replaced by Yuri Andropov.

1983

March 23—In a nationally televised address, Reagan announces plans to build the Strategic Defense Initiative (Star Wars) weapons system.

October 23—A terrorist truck bomb explodes at U.S. Marine headquarters in Beirut, Lebanon, killing over 225 Americans.

December 12—Terrorists bomb U.S., French, and other embassies in Kuwait.

1984

April—Secretary of Health and Human Services Margaret Heckler announces that the virus that causes AIDS has been isolated.

June 25—U.S. Senate passes resolution cutting off all aid to the Nicaraguan contras.

November 6—Reagan and Bush are reelected in a landslide victory.

1985

March 11—Mikhail Gorbachev becomes leader of the Soviet Union.

July 13—The Live Aid concert, held simultaneously in London and Philadelphia, raises almost $70 million for starving people in Africa.

November 19–20—Reagan and Gorbachev meet for the first time in Geneva, Switzerland, and plan for more meetings in the future.

1986

January 20—Martin Luther King Jr. Day is first celebrated as an official national holiday.

January 28—The space shuttle *Challenger* explodes after takeoff, killing all seven crew members.

February—Mikhail Gorbachev calls for radical reform of the Soviet economy, and speaks out against abuses of power within the Communist Party.

April 26—Explosion occurs at the nuclear power plant in the Ukraine city of Chernobyl.

September 14—President and Nancy Reagan, in joint news conference, announce "national crusade" against drugs.

October 11–12—Reagan and Gorbachev meet at summit in Reykjavik, Iceland, but reach no agreements.

November 6—The first reports of the Iran-contra affair begin to surface.

November 14—Ivan Boesky is fined $100 million and sentenced to prison for insider trading.

November 26—The Tower Commission is appointed to investigate the Iran-contra affair.

1987
May 5—Iran-contra hearings begin.

May 31—President Reagan calls for widespread testing in his first speech on AIDS.

October 19—The stock market crashes on what becomes known as "Black Monday." The Dow Jones plunges 508 points, the worst single-day decline in its history.

December 8—At a summit in Washington, D.C., Reagan and Gorbachev sign the Intermediate-range Nuclear Forces (INF) Treaty, the first in which the two superpowers commit to dismantling an entire class of nuclear missiles.

1988
February 4—U.S. grand jury indicts Panamanian leader Manuel Noriega on drug charges.

May 29–June 2—Reagan visits Moscow for the fourth summit meeting between the two leaders.

November 8—George Bush wins presidential election over Michael Dukakis.

1989
March 24—*Exxon Valdez* runs aground in Alaska, spilling millions of barrels of oil into the Prince William Sound.

May 4—Colonel Oliver North convicted on charges stemming from Iran-contra affair. The conviction is later overturned.

June 4—Chinese troops crush prodemocracy student protests in Tiananmen Square, Beijing.

June 5—The first democratic election in Poland in forty years brings an end to Communist rule in that country. Many Communist candidates are beaten by candidates from the prodemocracy Solidarity movement.

July—Gorbachev announces that Eastern European countries are free to decide their own political futures.

October 17—Massive earthquake strikes San Francisco.

November 9—East Germany opens its borders with West Germany, and celebrators begin tearing down the Berlin Wall. Between October 1989 and January 1990, the Communist governments of Czechoslovakia, Hungary, East Germany, Romania, and Bulgaria are all toppled.

December 20—U.S. forces invade Panama and capture dictator Manuel Noriega, who surrenders on January 3, 1990.

1990
February 11—Nelson Mandela, antiapartheid activist and leader of the African National Congress, is released from prison in South Africa.

April 24—Michael Milken, millionaire junk bond trader, pleads guilty to criminal charges.

August 2—Iraq invades Kuwait, and on August 7 President Bush sends U.S. troops to Saudi Arabia.

1991
June 17—Legal foundation of apartheid repealed by South Africa's parliament.

July 1—Warsaw Pact formally comes to an end.

August 19–29—After a failed coup attempt against Mikhail Gorbachev, Boris Yeltsin comes to power and the Communist Party is disbanded.

December 25—Gorbachev resigns as president of the Soviet Union. The following day, the union formally dissolves.

For Further Reading

AIDS

Elinor Burkett, *The Gravest Show on Earth: America in the Age of AIDS*. New York: Houghton Mifflin, 1995.

Steven Epstein, *Impure Science: AIDS, Activism, and the Politics of Knowledge*. Berkeley and Los Angeles: University of California Press, 1996.

Michael Fumento, *The Myth of Heterosexual AIDS*. Washington, DC: Regnery, 1993.

James Kinsella, *Covering the Plague: AIDS and the American Media*. New Brunswick, NJ: Rutgers University Press, 1989.

Randy Shilts, *And the Band Played on: Politics, People, and the AIDS Epidemic*. New York: St. Martin's Press, 1987.

America in the 1980s

Haynes Johnson, *Sleepwalking Through History: America in the Reagan Years*. New York: Anchor Books, 1992.

Peter B. Levy, *Encyclopedia of the Reagan-Bush Years*. Westport, CT: Greenwood Press, 1996.

Myron A. Marty, *Daily Life in the United States, 1960–1990: Decades of Discord*. Westport, CT: Greenwood Press, 1997.

Ellen Meltzer and Marc Aronson, *Day by Day: The Eighties*. New York: Facts On File, 1995.

Michael Schaller, *Reckoning with Reagan: America and Its President in the 1980s*. New York: Oxford University Press, 1992.

Gilbert T. Sewall, ed., *The Eighties: A Reader*. Reading, MA: Addison-Wesley, 1997.

David Wright, *America in the 20th Century: 1980–1989*. New York: Marshall Cavendish, 1995.

America in the Twentieth Century

Michael Barone, *Our Country: The Shaping of America from Roosevelt to Reagan*. New York: Free Press, 1990.

William H. Chafe, *The Unfinished Journey: America Since World War II*. New York: Oxford University Press, 1991.

Harold Evans, *The American Century*. New York: Alfred A. Knopf, 1998.

John E. Findling and Frank W. Thackeray, *Events That Changed America in the Twentieth Century*. Westport, CT: Greenwood Press, 1996.

Godfrey Hodgson. *The World Turned Right Side Up: A History of the Conservative Ascendancy in America*. New York: Houghton Mifflin, 1996.

Arthur S. Link, William A. Link, and William B. Catton, *American Epoch: A History of the United States Since 1900, Volume II: An Era of War and Uncertain Peace 1936–1985*. New York: Alfred A. Knopf, 1987.

George Moss, *America in the Twentieth Century*. Englewood Cliffs, NJ: Prentice-Hall, 1997.

Howard Zinn, *A People's History of the United States, 1492–Present*. New York: HarperCollins, 1995.

George Bush

George Bush and Brent Scowcroft, *A World Transformed*. New York: Alfred A. Knopf, 1998.

Dilys M. Hill and Phil Williams, eds., *The Bush Presidency: Triumphs and Adversities*. New York: St. Martin's Press, 1994.

David Mervin, *George Bush and the Guardianship Presidency*. New York: St. Martin's Press, 1996.

Herbert S. Parmet, *George Bush: The Life of a Lone Star Yankee*. New York: Scribner, 1997.

Kenneth W. Thompson, ed., *The Bush Presidency: Ten Intimate Perspectives of George Bush*. Lanham, MD: University Press of America, 1998.

The Cold War

Wesley M. Bagby, *America's International Relations Since World War I*. New York: Oxford University Press, 1999.

Michael R. Beschloss and Strobe Talbott, *At the Highest Levels: The Inside Story of the End of the Cold War*. Boston: Little, Brown, 1993.

Peter Cipkowski, *Revolution in Eastern Europe*. New York: John Wiley & Sons, 1991.

John Lewis Gaddis, *We Know Now: Rethinking Cold War History*. New York: Oxford University Press, 1998.

Michael Kort, *The Columbia Guide to the Cold War*. New York: Columbia University Press, 1998.

Walter LaFeber, *America, Russia, and the Cold War, 1945–1996*. New York: McGraw-Hill, 1997.

Ralph B. Levering, *The Cold War: A Post–Cold War History*. Wheeling, IL: Harlan Davidson, 1994.

John W. Mason, *The Cold War: 1945–1991*. London and New York: Routledge, 1996.

Dan Oberdorfer, *From the Cold War to a New Era: The United States and the Soviet Union, 1983–1991*. Baltimore: Johns Hopkins University Press, 1998.

Joseph Smith, *The Cold War*. Malden, MA: Blackwell, 1998.

Gale Stokes, *The Walls Came Tumbling Down: The Collapse of Communism in Eastern Europe*. New York: Oxford University Press, 1993.

Ralph Summy and Michael E. Salla, eds., *Why the Cold War Ended: A Range of Interpretations*. Westport, CT: Greenwood Press, 1995.

Martin Walker, *The Cold War: A History*. New York: Henry Holt, 1993.

Entertainment and Culture

Jonathan Bernstein, *Pretty in Pink: The Golden Age of Teenage Movies*. New York: St. Martin's Press, 1997.

Douglas Brode, *The Films of the Eighties*. New York: Carol Publishing Group, 1990.

Anthony Decurtis et al., *The Rolling Stone Illustrated History of Rock & Roll*. New York: Random House, 1992.

Linda K. Fuller, *The Cosby Show: Audiences, Impact, and Implications*. Westport, CT: Greenwood Press, 1992.

Susan Jeffords, *Hard Bodies: Hollywood Masculinity in the Reagan Era*. New Brunswick, NJ: Rutgers University Press, 1994.

Richard A. Johnson, *American Fads*. New York: Beech Tree Books, 1985.

Tom McGrath, *MTV: The Making of a Revolution*. Philadelphia: Running Press, 1992.

William J. Palmer, *The Films of the Eighties: A Social History*. Illinois: Southern Illinois University Press, 1993.

Neil Postman, *Amusing Ourselves to Death: Public Discourse in the Age of Show Business*. New York: Viking Press, 1985.

Matthew Rettenmund, *Totally Awesome 80s: A Lexicon of the Music, Videos, Movies, TV Shows, Stars, and Trends of That Decadent Decade*. New York: St. Martin's Press, 1996.

David Szatmary, *Rockin' in Time: A Social History of Rock-and-Roll*. Englewood Cliffs, NJ: Prentice-Hall, 1996.

Ronald Reagan

Dinesh D'Souza, *Ronald Reagan: How an Ordinary Man Became an Extraordinary Leader*. New York: Free Press, 1997.

Peter Kornbluh and Malcolm Byrne, eds., *The Iran-Contra Scandal: The Declassified History*. New York: New Press, 1992.

Edwin Meese, *With Reagan: The Inside Story*. Washington, DC: Regnery, 1992.

Edmund Morris, *Dutch: A Memoir of Ronald Reagan*. New York: Random House, 1999.

William E. Pemberton, *Exit with Honor: The Life and Presidency of Ronald Reagan*. Armonk, NY: M.E. Sharpe, 1997.

Ronald Reagan, *An American Life*. New York: Simon & Schuster, 1990.

Bob Schieffer and Gary Paul Gates, *The Acting President: Ronald Reagan and the Men Who Helped Him Create the Illusion That Held America Spellbound*. New York: Dutton, 1989.

Mary E. Stuckey, *The President as Interpreter-in-Chief*. Chatham, NJ: Chatham House, 1991.

Kenneth T. Walsh, *Ronald Reagan: Biography*. New York: Random House, 1997.

Lawrence E. Walsh, *Firewall: The Iran-Contra Conspiracy and Cover-Up*. New York: W.W. Norton, 1997.

Technology and the Environment in the 1980s

Martin Campbell-Kelly and William Aspray, *Computer: A History of the Information Machine*. New York: HarperCollins, 1997.

Paul E. Ceruzzi, *A History of Modern Computing*. Cambridge, MA: MIT Press, 1998.

Calus Jensen, *No Downlink: A Dramatic Narrative About the Challenger Accident and Our Time*. New York: Farrar, Straus & Giroux, 1996.

John Keeble, *Out of the Channel: The Exxon Valdez Oil Spill in Prince William Sound*. Cheney, WA: Eastern Washington University Press, 1999.

Sandra Markle, *After the Spill: The Exxon Valdez Disaster, Then and Now*. New York: Walker, 1999.

Malcolm McConnell, *Challenger: A Major Malfunction*. Garden City, NY: Doubleday, 1987.

Zhores A. Medvedev, *The Legacy of Chernobyl*. New York: W.W. Norton, 1990.

Mary Northrup, *American Computer Pioneers*. Springfield, NJ: Enslow, 1998.

Piers Paul Read, *Ablaze: The Story of the Heroes and Victims of Chernobyl*. New York: Random House, 1993.

Wall Street and the 1980s Economy

Kathleen Day, *S&L Hell: The People and the Politics Behind the $1 Trillion Savings and Loan Scandal*. New York: W.W. Norton, 1993.

Michael Lewis, *The Money Culture*. New York: W.W. Norton, 1991.

Richard B. McKenzie, *What Went Right in the 1980s*. San Francisco: Pacific Research Institute for Public Policy, 1994.

Nicolaus Mills, ed., *Culture in an Age of Money: The Legacy of the 1980s in America*. Chicago: I.R. Dee, 1990.

Kevin Phillips, *The Politics of Rich and Poor: Wealth and the American Electorate in the Reagan Aftermath*. New York: Random House, 1990.

James Brewer Stewart, *Den of Thieves*. New York: Simon & Schuster, 1991.

Index